Small States in Transition: from Vulnerability to Competitiveness

Ganeshan Wignaraja
Marlon Lezama
David Joiner

THE COMMONWEALTH SECRETARIAT

Commonwealth Secretariat
Marlborough House
Pall Mall, London SW1Y 5HX, United Kingdom

© Commonwealth Secretariat, 2004

All rights reserved. No part of this publication may be reproduced, stored in a retrieval system, or transmitted in any form or by any means, electronic or mechanical, including photocopying, recording or otherwise without the permission of the publisher.

Designed and published by the Commonwealth Secretariat
Printed in Britain by Formara Ltd.

Wherever possible, the Commonwealth Secretariat uses paper sourced from sustainable forests or from sources that minimise a destructive impact on the environment.

ISBN 0-85092-802-8   Price: £10.99

Web site: http//www.thecommonwealth.org

The Authors

Dr. Ganesh Wignaraja, at the time of undertaking the study, was Head of Competitiveness Strategy and SME Development at Maxwell Stamp Plc and a Visiting Fellow at the UN Institute for New Technologies in Maastricht. He has since taken up a senior appointment at the Asian Development Bank and is the lead consultant on this Small States Study.

Marlon Lezama is Chief Programme Officer (Trade), Special Advisory Services Division (SASD) of the Commonwealth Secretariat and Team Leader of the Small States Study. He is responsible for developing, implementing and managing a range of trade-related technical assistance programmes for Commonwealth developing countries.

David Joiner is a Senior Economist at Maxwell Stamp Plc, specialising in trade policy and enterprise development. He was formerly an Overseas Development Institute Fellow at the Pacific Islands Forum Secretariat.

Acknowledgements

This study was undertaken as part of Commonwealth Secretariat's ongoing trade-related technical assistance activities to small states. It focuses on the measurement of the industrial competitiveness record in small states and the public policies they could adopt to improve their performance. The study will be of interest to all those concerned in the adjustment of small states and their enterprises to accelerating globalisation. It will be of particular interest to policy-makers, international donor organisations, academics and researchers, business organisations and students.

The Commonwealth Fund for Technical Cooperation financed the study and the authors are most grateful for its support. They are also grateful to the Commonwealth Secretariat's Special Advisory Services Division and Economic Affairs Division for constant encouragement and other assistance; to the Mauritius Industrial Development Agency for facilitating a mission to Mauritius; to the Tourism and Industrial Development Company for organising a mission to Trinidad and Tobago; to the International Trade Centre (ITC) UNCTAD/WTO for facilitating a mission to Geneva; and to Clare Groves and Geoff Kebbell for able research assistance. Thanks are also due to the numerous individuals, enterprises and officials in these countries who gave us their views and insights. Preliminary findings of the study were presented at the Joint Commonwealth Secretariat/ITC Executive Forum on 'Small States in Transition: From Vulnerability to Competitiveness' held in Port of Spain, 18–21 January 2004. The authors are grateful to participants for comments and suggestions. The authors bear sole responsibility for the views expressed in this study.

Contents

Executive Summary ix

1 Introduction 1
1.1. Context and Purpose of the Study 1
1.2 The New Policy Focus: Competitiveness as well as Vulnerability 3
1.3 Outline of the Study 7

2 Understanding Competitiveness in a Global World 11
2.1 The Importance of Knowledge in Globalisation 11
2.2 Diverse Perspectives on Competitiveness 13
2.3 Enterprise-level Learning and Competitiveness 15
2.4 Role of Policies and Institutions 19

3 Measuring the Performance of Small States 23
3.1 Introduction 23
3.2 Current Benchmarking Initiatives and Their Appropriateness for Small States 23
3.3 A Small States Specific Competitiveness Index 28
3.3.1 Country-level Findings 28
3.3.2 Findings by Region, Income Group and Country Size 34
3.3.3 Comparison with Results from Other Indices 38
3.4 Explaining Industrial Competitiveness Performance 38
3.4.1 T-Test and Variables 39
3.4.2 The T-Test Results 40
3.4.3 Linear Regression Analysis 43
Appendix 3.1: Construction of the SSMECI 45

4 Mauritius 49
4.1 Initial Conditions and Industrial Achievements 49
4.2 Explaining Industrial Success 52
4.3 Institutional Support 56
4.4 Structural Constraints and Upgrading 59
4.5 Recent Competitiveness Initiatives 61
4.6 Lessons from Mauritius 63

5	**Trinidad and Tobago**	65
5.1	Initial Conditions and Industrial Achievements	65
5.2	Selected Enterprise Cases	67
5.3	Policy and Institutional Factors	70
5.3.1	*Policy Framework*	*70*
5.3.2	*Current SME and Trade Support Institutions*	*72*
5.4	Lessons from Trinidad and Tobago	75
6	**Agenda for Enhancing Competitiveness**	77
6.1	Principles Underlying an Agenda	77
6.1.1	*Focus on Evolving Comparative Advantage*	*77*
6.1.2	*Tailor to National Circumstances*	*78*
6.1.3	*Link with Regional Markets and Institutions*	*78*
6.1.4	*Combine Incentive and Supply-side Measures*	*79*
6.1.5	*Involve All Major Stakeholders*	*79*
6.1.6	*Prioritise Interventions and Actions*	*80*
6.2	An Illustrative Agenda	80
6.2.1	*Types of Policy Instrument and Support Measures*	*80*
6.2.2	*Example Agenda*	*81*
6.3	An Implementation Road Map	82
6.4	Conditions for Success	88
6.5	A Last Word	91

Bibliography   94

Boxes

1.1	What is a Small State?	2
1.2	Economic Benefits from Enhancing Competitiveness in Small States	6
2.1	The Knowledge-driven Global Economy and Small States	12
2.2	Defining Industrial Competitiveness in Small Developing States	14
2.3	Building Competitive Capabilities in African SMEs	16
2.4	Gaps in NIS in Small States and All Developing Countries	21
3.1	Small States Manufactured Export Competitiveness Index	29
3.2	Some Determinants of Malta's Success	32
4.1	The Importance of the Textile and Clothing Industry in Mauritius	51
4.2	Mauritius's Outward-looking Trade and Investment Strategy	54
5.1	Strategy, Technical Innovation and Training the Key to Success – Soft Drinks Company S. M. Jaleel & Co.	67
5.2	Trinidad's Own Multinational – Angostura	69

Figures

2.1	The Enterprise-level Learning Process	16
2.2	National Innovation System	20
4.1	Manufacturing FDI Inflows (US$ million), 1985–2002	60
6.1	Competitiveness Strategy Implementation – A Road Map	86
6.2	Conditions for Success	89

Tables

1.1	Basic Profile of Small States, Most Recent Estimates	8
3.1	Features of Recent Competitiveness Indices	24
3.2	Summary of Results from MECI	27
3.3	Country Rankings for the Three Separate Variables	30
3.4	Overall SSMECI Ranking	30
3.5	SSMECI Performance by Region	35
3.6	SSMECI Performance by Income Group	37
3.7	SSMECI Performance by Population Size Group	37
3.8	Comparison of Results from SSMECI, MECI and WEF Indices	38
3.9	*T*-Tests to Examine the Significance of Determinants	41
3.10	Linear Regression Analysis with Dependent Variable, SSMECI	44
A3.1	Precise Sources of all Data in SSMECI	46
4.1	Selected Indicators, 1970, and Most Recent Estimates (MRE)	50
4.2	Inflows of Total FDI in Selected Economies, 1985–95 ($ million and percentage of Gross Domestic Investment)	52
4.3	Overview of Institutions Supporting Enterprises (MRE)	57
4.4	Manufactured Export Growth, 1980–2002 (annual average percentage per year)	61
5.1	Comparative Statistics for Trinidad and Tobago – Before Structural Adjustment and Most Recent Estimates	66
6.1	A Policy Matrix for Small States	83

Executive Summary

Globalisation is a powerful influence on the future competitiveness of enterprises in the world's smallest economies. On the one hand, it offers small states' enterprises access to new technologies, new skills, new markets, new financial sources and hence better outward-oriented growth prospects than ever before. But on the other hand, it exposes them to intensive competition from imports, foreign investment and low-cost developing country enterprises. There is a real prospect that there will be winners and losers among small states and the enterprises within them. The double-edged nature of globalisation seems somewhat daunting, both to policy-makers and to enterprises in small states.

Against this background, this study deals with a pressing economic policy question facing the world's smallest economies: how can small states enhance industrial competitiveness and alleviate economic vulnerabilities associated with small country size? There is a widespread perception that small country size (i.e. economies with 1.5 million people or less) hinders the achievement of industrial competitiveness. This study seeks to address this issue. The transition from vulnerability to competitiveness is at the forefront of current economic policy debates in small states. There is still little sign of consensus about the way forward.

In an attempt to shed some light on these important policy issues, this study addresses four inter-related questions:

- What is the meaning of competitiveness in relation to small states and their enterprises?

- What is the recent industrial competitiveness experience of small states with globalisation and what factors determine success at a cross-country level?

- What kinds of enterprise strategies, policies and institutions have been adopted by small states which have succeeded?

- What principles, actors and measures might underpin the development of future industrial competitiveness policies for other small states?

Competitiveness is often a difficult concept to understand, analyse and apply, even in the context of developed economies, with fully developed institutions, limited market failures and extensive data. These problems are exacerbated when dealing with small states, which typically have underdeveloped institutions and lack available data. Therefore, in order to analyse industrial competitiveness in small states a simple framework has been developed (Chapter 2). This draws on recent literature on technology and innovation in developing countries, and underlines the dynamic links between technology, firms, industries, policies and institutions in developing competitiveness in small states. It emphasises that competitiveness arises at the level of the firm, but also stresses the importance of national-level factors like a supportive policy framework and the quality of institutions.

To explore the recent performance of small states in relation to competitiveness, a Small States Manufactured Export Competitiveness Index (SSMECI) has been developed to benchmark industrial competitiveness (Chapter 3). To the best of our knowledge, this represents the first attempt to provide a comprehensive picture of the competitiveness performance of small states. It found that the performance of small states varies significantly across geographical regions, income groups and country size classes, and real performance patterns can be observed. Unsurprisingly, Europe was the best performing region, with Malta and Estonia occupying the top two positions in the index. Small states in southern Africa were the next most successful, with Mauritius and the four BLNS states (Botswana, Lesotho, Namibia and Swaziland) all in the top 11 of the index, but performance in the Pacific and West Africa was poor. Even within the small states sample, size was found to be important, with larger small states performing better than micro-states on average. In order to interpret the underlying determinants of competitiveness performance in small states, statistical analysis was used to see which determinants have an influence on SSMECI rankings. This showed that macro fundamentals, such as interest rates, were positive factors, as were external influences such as foreign direct investment (FDI). Diversification of exports was important to good performance, as was a strong base of human capital.

In order to explore the kinds of enterprise strategies, policies and institutions that have been adopted by successful small states, two countries were selected for further study. Both in the top five of the SSMECI, Mauritius (fourth) and Trinidad and Tobago (fifth) are examples of small states that have been successful, despite significantly different initial conditions and paths to success.

Mauritius (Chapter 4) is one of the few small states to have successfully broken into the production of manufactures for export (mainly textiles and garments) and is further attempting to diversify into services exports. In the last 30 years, this small state went from being a poor monocrop producer to an aspiring newly industrialising economy. Traditional economic sectors like sugar exports and up-market tourism laid the foundations for modern Mauritian industrial development by providing a surplus for investment and an international country reputation for producing quality goods and services. The real engine of growth, however, was export-oriented FDI in export processing zones (EPZs), particularly in textiles and garments. Several factors seem to explain why FDI came to Mauritius. These include an outward-looking trade and investment strategy; preferential market access to the EU; cheap and bilingual labour; investment in human capital; political and macroeconomic stability; relatively efficient government; and comprehensive institutional support. Its outward-looking trade and investment strategy emphasised the establishment of public and private EPZs, investment incentives, access to duty-free raw materials and investor facilitation. With a recent slowing down of FDI, Mauritius has developed a new competitiveness strategy in order to sustain its competitiveness and diversify its economic base away from a dependence on textiles and garments. Among other things, it is attempting to better target foreign investment into the services sector, promote small and medium enterprise (SME) development, upgrade tertiary level technical skills and improve its infrastructure, particularly information and communications technology (ICT). Mauritius' competitiveness experience offers valuable lessons for other small economies.

Trinidad and Tobago (Chapter 5) is today the most industrialised of the Caribbean small states and the highest ranking in the SSMECI index in the Caribbean region. To a large degree this reflects its endowment of natural resources, and the significant oil and natural gas downstream industries that have developed from this resource. However, the reasons for success run deeper than this, and all small states can learn lessons from Trinidad's experience of providing a policy environment which supports competitive growth, of managing natural resources well (whether they be petroleum based or not), and of leveraging from this to diversify the industrial base. After a crisis in the early 1980s caused by over-reliance on oil, a stable, well thought out policy has been the cornerstone of Trinidad's recent success. The macroeconomic fundamental conditions have been well managed. Focus has been put on an outward-orientated trade and investment strategy with well-focused export incentive policies and institutions developed to support enterprise growth and export development, such as the Tourism and Industrial Development Company (TIDCO). Trinidad and Tobago has also made conscious efforts to develop its human resource base and its infrastructure. A case study of an enterprise success story in Trinidad shows that an SME in a non-oil related sector (beverages) can become a world player and be globally competitive in the space of 20 years, despite the 'handicap' of its small state origins.

The cross-country analysis and the case studies of Mauritius and Trinidad and Tobago suggested that a coherent competitiveness strategy is an important ingredient of success in a small state. Six important principles underlie the formulation of such a strategy:

- A focus on evolving comparative advantage;

- Tailoring policy to national circumstances;

- Linkages with regional markets and institutions;

- Combining incentives and supply-side measures;

- Involvement of all major stakeholders;

- Prioritisation of interventions and actions.

A wide range of policy instruments and support measures can be included in a competitiveness strategy in a small state. An example agenda, with 47 initiatives, is provided in the study for a typical small state (Chapter 6). While detailed measures and support measures need to be country specific, the main strategic thrusts can be identified as follows:

- Maintain credible macroeconomic policies and exchange rate flexibility;
- Persist with outward-oriented trade policies;
- Foster small business start-up and growth;
- Invest in human resources;
- Ensure adequate technological support;
- Encourage and increase inflows of foreign direct investment;
- Improve private sector associations;
- Strengthen public–private sector dialogue and partnerships;
- Promote e-commerce and e-government;
- Improve the quality and coverage of infrastructure.

The process of tailoring competitiveness strategy to a given small state can be guided by a simple road map. An example of a road map is provided in Chapter 6 consisting of four phases, each building on previous efforts: inception review, assessing competitiveness, designing strategy and sustaining competitiveness.

A coherent competitiveness strategy, together with a good implementation plan, is a necessary but not sufficient condition for long-run export success in small states. The economic development record of small states suggests that other factors are required to support even the best-designed competitiveness strategies. These include external factors which originate outside an economy (such as financial crises, natural disasters and terrorism) which are largely outside the scope of policy-making. Another category of factors are internal to a small economy and can be influenced by national policy-making. Many of these issues (political stability, government capabilities and the development of a policy consensus with the private sector and other interested parties) fall under the heading of governance, which is a separate topic that requires further analysis for small states.

Small states face many challenges in the global economy, and size is definitely a constraint. However, despite these challenges, there are success stories among the small states. Rather than concentrating purely on vulnerability, many small states would benefit from a more proactive approach to improving competitiveness through concerted policy action. There are no magic wands in economic development, and achieving success will take years of hard work, but small states that tackle the constraints identified and design and implement a coherent competitiveness strategy appear to have the best chance of long-term success.

1

Introduction

1.1 Context and Purpose of the Study

This study deals with a pressing economic policy question facing the world's smallest economies: how can small states enhance their industrial competitiveness and alleviate the economic vulnerabilities associated with small country size? There is a widespread perception that small size (i.e. economies with 1.5 million people or less) hinders the achievement of industrial competitiveness. This study seeks to address this issue. The transition from vulnerability to competitiveness is at the forefront of current economic policy debates in small states. To date there is little sign of consensus about the way forward.

These debates centre on the economic consequences of rapid globalisation (see, for instance, Bernal, 2001; Matsis, 2001; Treebhoohun, 2001). Interestingly, the positive aspects of globalisation – notably, access to new technologies and markets – appear to receive relatively little attention. Instead, policy-makers are deeply concerned about the decline of domestic enterprises and even industrial marginalisation in an open, integrated world economy. Prominent too are worries about rising unemployment, poverty, crime and related social problems. Globalisation is associated with demanding international markets, falling trade barriers, increasing technological progress, inflows of foreign investment and movement of people. Many small states have adopted economic reform programmes to enable enterprises to adjust to the new international environment. However, the limited supply response from domestic enterprises has led to disillusionment with economic reform and has fuelled fears of industrial marginalisation.

A search for policy options to deal with globalisation has also begun in some small states. Attempts to reverse globalisation through new barriers to imports and foreign investment are largely ruled out. As a result, there is growing interest in policies to improve industrial competitiveness within an open economy paradigm.

This study is based on the premise that globalisation is irreversible and that while country size may be a constraint, it is not an insurmountable barrier to improving competitiveness. Small states have to adopt appropriate measures to realise the gains from international integration, reduce its negative effects and address issues related to country size. Accordingly, small states will need to put in place coherent competitiveness policies to support industrial restructuring; this study seeks to contribute to their development. With international development experience pointing to the limited value of a one-size-fits-all competitiveness policy regime, the study underlines the need to tailor measures to the individual national circumstances of small states and the nature of the enterprises

Box 1.1: What is a Small State?

There are many ways (for example GDP and population) to define a small state. Following the Commonwealth Secretariat (1997), this study defines a small state as an economy with 1.5 million people or less. Accordingly, in this study 47 Commonwealth and non-Commonwealth countries are considered to be small states, along with four somewhat larger states which share many of the physical and economic characteristics of small states in their respective regions (see Table 1.1 for population data). This group also includes a subset of economies (with a population of 200,000 or less) that can be considered micro-states. Such economies face many of the same problems that affect larger small states as well as additional problems arising from their tiny size.

The 47 small state sample is presented below by geographical region and Commonwealth membership (Commonwealth members are shown in italics and the four countries with populations of over 1.5 million are shown in bold type).

Small States by Geographical Region

AFRICA: *Botswana*, Cape Verde, Comoros, Djibouti, Equatorial Guinea, Gabon, *The Gambia*, Guinea-Bissau, **Lesotho**, **Namibia**, São Tomé and Príncipe, *Swaziland* (12)

CARIBBEAN: *Antigua and Barbuda*, *Bahamas*, *Barbados*, *Belize*, *Dominica*, *Grenada*, *Guyana*, *Jamaica*, *St Kitts and Nevis*, *St Lucia*, *St Vincent and the Grenadines*, Suriname, *Trinidad and Tobago* (13)

PACIFIC: Federated States of Micronesia, *Fiji Islands*, *Kiribati*, Marshall Islands, *Nauru*, Palau, **Papua New Guinea**, *Samoa*, *Solomon Islands*, *Tonga*, *Tuvalu*, *Vanuatu* (12)

INDIAN OCEAN: *Maldives*, *Mauritius*, *Seychelles* (3)

OTHER ASIA: Bahrain, Bhutan, *Brunei*, Qatar (4)

EUROPE AND MEDITERRANEAN: *Cyprus*, Estonia, *Malta* (3)

Small States by Commonwealth Membership

COMMONWEALTH STATES: Botswana, The Gambia, Lesotho, Namibia, Swaziland, Antigua and Barbuda, Bahamas, Barbados, Belize, Dominica, Grenada, Guyana, Jamaica, St Kitts and Nevis, St Lucia, St Vincent and the Grenadines, Trinidad and Tobago, Fiji Islands, Kiribati, Nauru, Papua New Guinea, Samoa, Solomon Islands, Tonga, Tuvalu, Vanuatu, Maldives, Mauritius, Seychelles, Brunei, Cyprus Malta (32)

NON-COMMONWEALTH STATES: Cape Verde, Comoros, Djibouti, Equatorial Guinea, Gabon, Guinea-Bissau, São Tomé and Príncipe, Suriname, Federated States of Micronesia, Marshall Islands, Palau, Bahrain, Bhutan, Qatar, Estonia (15) within them. However, preparation of a detailed diagnostic analysis of the industrial competitiveness record, relevant determinants and specific recommendations for individual small states is beyond the scope of this exercise.[1] Those with specific national and sectoral expertise may more meaningfully do this task at country level.

The present study has a more limited goal: to provide insights into what works (and what does not) in terms of industrial competitiveness policy for small states by synthesising conceptual work, available empirical evidence and lessons drawn from successful cases. Apart from stocktaking, it sets the stage for thinking about a more comprehensive competitiveness policy framework for small states than traditional economic reform programmes. This framework may be more appropriate to competitiveness because it derives from micro-level theories of technical change and enterprise restructuring rather than macroeconomics *per se*. It also highlights additional policy measures to those of standard economic reform programmes, as well as roles for key public and private sector actors in policy formulation and implementation. Hence, the study may be a useful input into both national competitiveness policy exercises in small states and international policy dialogues with bilateral aid donors and multilateral agencies. It may also be of interest to researchers and students concerned with competitiveness, private sector development and post-adjustment strategy issues in small states.

The study addresses four inter-related questions:

- What is the meaning of competitiveness in relation to a small state and its enterprises?

- What is the recent industrial competitiveness experience of small states with globalisation and what factors determine success at a cross-country level?

- What kinds of enterprise strategies, policies and institutions have been adopted by successful small states?

- What principles, actors and measures might underpin the development of future industrial competitiveness policies for other small states?

1.2 The New Policy Focus: Competitiveness as well as Vulnerability

This study of competitiveness in small states comes at a time when the current focus of research and policy attention is on the economic vulnerability of small states. For many years small states, as part of larger developing country groupings, have enjoyed preferential market access, high levels of grant-based foreign aid, longer adjustment periods to international agreements and other special policy measures. However, in recent years globalisation has reduced this preferential treatment, with Uruguay Round liberalisation eroding the coverage of trade preferences available to small states and foreign aid flows to small states declining. Developed countries have become increasingly focused on countries with high abject poverty, and preoccupied with their own interests such as the war on terrorism and domestic economic problems. If current trends continue, small states are likely to receive reduced foreign aid and less effective market access than ever before. The preferential treatment that is still available is often limited to least developed countries (LDCs) with high levels of abject poverty, a category for which few small states qualify.

In response to this, recent work has tried to show that small states do face specific problems and that their small size can specifically constrain economic development. Several studies highlight the existence of an inverse relationship between country size and susceptibility to economic, political and environmental risks and threats (Commonwealth Consultative Group, 1985; Commonwealth Secretariat, 1997; Streeten, 1993; Briguglio, 1995; Atkins et al., 2001; Grynberg, 2001; Collier and Dollar, 2001; Winters and Martins, 2003).[2] This literature concludes that small states are more vulnerable than larger economies for the following reasons.

1. They have higher exposure to external shocks because of higher trade openness which causes short-term instability in export earnings and domestic demand.

2. They have less access to international financial markets and concessionary finance due to a lack of creditworthiness.

3. Their transport costs are higher per unit value of goods transported due to their remoteness and the relatively small values of cargoes carried.

4. They are at a disadvantage in attracting foreign investment because they are rated to be significantly more risky.

5. They are dependent on a single product and face reductions in preferential market access due to trade liberalisation under international trade agreements.

6. They are more exposed to serious environmental risks (for example natural disasters, rises in sea-level and marine pollution) due to their geographical location and face large environmental bills.

In an effort to redress the current erosion of preferences and special treatment, arguments based on vulnerability have been taken up with great vigour by small states' representatives in international forums such as the WTO, the EU and the Commonwealth. Calls have been made to insert clauses into current and future trade and aid agreements to highlight the special circumstances of small states, and to provide for special treatment that would redress the current erosion of preferences. However, the outcome of such efforts to date – and the prospects for future success – is at best limited, and even if it were to improve significantly, the underlying trends of globalisation are unlikely to change. Realistically, small states will increasingly have to compete on world markets for exports and foreign investment, and will receive less in aid and special treatment.

This realistic, if slightly pessimistic, prediction has many macro- and microeconomic implications for small states, not all of which can be covered here. This study therefore focuses on the concept that in addition to looking at vulnerability, much more attention needs to be devoted to improving competitiveness in small states, so that they are in a better position to face this new economic environment – irrespective of preferential treatment. Such an argument is not intended to replace the vulnerability issue, which still needs to be pursued, particularly in micro-states, but rather to take a two-pronged approach to dealing with small states' development problems. As such it focuses on practical issues for policy-makers in small states that can be pursued independently and are not reliant on the results of lobbying and advocacy.

The economic imperative for adopting a new strategic focus on competitiveness in small states is reinforced by a growing body of literature on this subject which suggests that current performance is weak in small states. Cross-country and individual country studies highlight the following findings:

- *The relative importance of small states in world exports has declined since the 1950s.* The combined share of the total exports of 35 small states in total world exports fell from 1.2 per cent to 0.4 per cent in the period from the mid-1950s to 2000 (Razzaque, 2002). If the oil-rich small states are excluded, the decline is from 0.7 per cent to 0.2 per cent over the same period.

- *Small states have had weaker manufactured export growth rates and have more limited export sectors than large states.* An examination of 18 small states and 23 large states showed that only three small states (Mauritius, Trinidad and Tobago, and the Bahamas) achieved a respectable manufactured export growth rate of above 10 per cent per year during 1980–1993 and had a manufactured export base of over $0.5 billion (Wignaraja, 1997:37). Jamaica and Malta had manufactured export bases worth over $0.5 billion (1993) but recorded slower export growth rates.

- *Unfavourable external factors arising from the international economic environment – outside the influence of small states – help to explain some of their competitive weaknesses.* Many of these are well known in debates on small states. They include declining terms of trade for primary products relative to manufactures; fluctuating international demand; rising protectionism through non-tariff measures in export markets; and new WTO rules which raise market access requirements (Harris, 1997; Razzaque, 2002).

- Far more important to competitiveness, according to case studies, are *factors arising from the nature of the policy environment and other country-level conditions.* The cases of Jamaica and Mauritius highlight contrasting experiences. Jamaica's lagging manufactured export growth rate is in part attributed to unfavourable macroeconomic and political conditions, including high nominal interest rates, insufficient depreciation of the real exchange rate and gaps in export incentives (Harris, 1997; Wint, 2003).

Box 1.2: Economic Benefits from Enhancing Competitiveness in Small States

Competitiveness is by no means a development panacea for small economies but it can significantly contribute to economic development. Several potential economic benefits are associated with improving the competitiveness of enterprises in small economies. These include the following:

1. **Increased exports.** Firms with improved technological and marketing capabilities tend to export more of their output than less dynamic firms. This leads to increased exports and higher foreign exchange earnings.

2. **Faster growth and higher per capita income.** Improved export performance feeds through into faster economic growth via standard multiplier effects, improved resource allocation and dynamic effects of exporting. In turn, faster growth raises per capita income.

3. **More foreign investment.** Small economies with a strong base of internationally competitive domestic firms indicate a better policy environment for the private sector and a good base of suppliers. These conditions reduce the risks associated with foreign investment in small economies, which in turn helps to sustain competitiveness through access to markets, technologies and skills.

4. **Higher employment.** As they export and grow, competitive enterprises tend to increase their demand for labour. This increases employment and helps to reduce the persistent unemployment problems that affect many small states.

5. **Better education and health services.** An internationally competitive enterprise sector implies a high level of tax revenue (via corporation and personal income tax) and hence more resources for investment in schools, hospitals and other public services.

Meanwhile, Mauritius's success is attributed to inflows of export-oriented foreign investment, attracted by competitive investment incentives, cheap and literate labour, a relatively cost-competitive infrastructure and preferential market access to the European Union (World Bank, 1994; Lall and Wignaraja, 1998).

- Furthermore, it is argued that *small firms in small economies are at a major disadvantage compared to large firms in taking advantage of the new export and investment opportunities provided by globalisation* (Bernal, 2001). Small firms are said to find it difficult to attain internal economies of scale (where the unit cost is influenced by the size of firm) and external economies of scale (where unit cost depends on the size of the industry but not necessarily the size of the firm). They are also said to find it difficult to attain economies of scope (i.e. economies obtained by a firm using its existing resources, skills and technologies to create new products and/or services for export).

Given this poor performance, an effort to focus on competitiveness as well as vulnerability would be particularly pertinent, and would need to concentrate on enhancing the capacity of domestic enterprises, ensuring a supportive competitiveness policy framework and attracting foreign investment. The overall benefits of increased competitiveness to small states are highlighted in Box 1.2.

1.3 Outline of the Study

The remainder of the study is organised as follows.

Chapter 2 provides a simple framework for analysing industrial competitiveness in small states in a rapidly globalising international economy, drawing on recent literature on technology and innovation in developing countries. This framework underlines the dynamic links between technology, firms, industries, policies and institutions in developing competitiveness in small states. It emphasises that competitiveness arises at the level of the firm. The costly investment process involved in the absorption of imported technologies at the level of the firm and the effects of firms' collective learning on industrial competitiveness are highlighted. So too are the importance of national-level factors like a supportive policy framework and the quality of institutions.

Chapter 3 examines the industrial competitiveness experience of individual small states, as well as of geographical regions, income groups and country size classes. It benchmarks the industrial competitiveness of these categories using a Small States Manufactured Export Competitiveness Index and examines some determinants through statistical analysis. To the best of our knowledge, the SSMECI represents the first attempt to provide a comprehensive picture of the competitiveness performance of small states. Comparisons of our results with those of other competitiveness indices by the World Economic Forum (WEF), the International Institute for Management Development (IMD) and the UN Industrial Development Organisation (UNIDO) suggest that international efforts have concentrated on large states and little attention has been paid to small ones.

Chapters 4 and 5 deal with national and enterprise level competitiveness experiences in selected small states. Through case studies of Mauritius and Trinidad and Tobago, these chapters examine the importance of initial conditions, policies, institutional support and firm-level strategies in enhancing competitiveness in small states. Both economies are widely regarded as outliers in their respective regions, having achieved an impressive competitiveness performance. This perception is also confirmed by their relatively high SSMECI rankings.

Chapter 6 concludes with suggestions for enhancing the future competitiveness of small states. The emphasis is on the formulation of a proactive national competitiveness approach to dealing with the process of globalisation. The suggestions focus on the key roles to be played by enterprises themselves, as well as by governments and business associations.

Table 1.1: Basic Profile of Small States, Most Recent Estimates

Country	Population (2001)	GDP per capita (current US$ 2001)	GDP per capita (PPP US$ 2001)	HDI Rank (2003)[a]	HDI Value Index (2003)
Antigua and Barbuda	68,490	9,961	10,170	56	0.798
Bahamas	309,840	15,550	16,270	49	0.812
Bahrain	651,000	12,189	16,060	37	0.839
Barbados	268,190	10,281	15,560	27	0.888
Belize	247,110	3,258	5,690	67	0.776
Bhutan	828,040	637	1,833	136	0.511
Botswana	1,695,000	3,066	7,820	125	0.614
Brunei	344,000	14,088	19,210	31	0.872
Cape Verde	446,400	1,264	5,570	103	0.727
Comoros	571,890	386	1,870	134	0.528
Cyprus	760,650	12,004	21,190	25	0.891
Djibouti	644,330	894	2,370	153	0.462
Dominica	71,870	3,607	5,520	68	0.776
Equatorial Guinea	469,090	3,935	15,073	116	0.664
Estonia	1,364,000	4,051	10,170	41	0.833
Fiji Islands	817,000	2,062	4,850	81	0.754
Gabon	1,260,790	3,437	5,990	118	0.653
Gambia, The	1,340,770	291	2,050	151	0.463
Grenada	100,410	3,965	6,740	93	0.738
Guinea-Bissau	1,225,620	162	970	166	0.373
Guyana	766,260	912	4,690	92	0.740
Jamaica	2,590,000	3,005	3,720	78	0.757
Kiribati	92,810	430	–	–	–
Lesotho	2,061,730	386	2,420	137	0.510
Maldives	280,320	2,229	4,798	86	0.751
Malta	395,000	9,150	13,160	33	0.856
Marshall Islands	52,500	1,937	–	–	–
Mauritius	1,200,000	3,771	9,860	62	0.779
Micronesia, Federated States of	120,230	1,914	–	–	–
Namibia	1,792,060	1,730	7,120	124	0.627
Nauru	10,000	–	–	–	–
Palau	19,500	6,280		–	–
Papua New Guinea	5,252,530	552	2,570	132	0.548
Qatar	597,550	27,536	19,844	44	0.826
Samoa	174,000	1,404	6,180	70	0.775
São Tomé & Príncipe	151,100	311	1,317	122	0.639
Seychelles	82,420	6,912	17,030	36	0.840
Solomon Islands	430,760	683	1,910	123	0.632
St Kitts and Nevis	45,050	7,609	11,300	51	0.808

Table 1.1 (continued)

Country	Population (2001)	GDP per capita (current US$ 2001)	GDP per capita (PPP US$ 2001)	HDI Rank (2003)[a]	HDI Value Index (2003)
St Lucia	156,700	4,222	5,260	71	0.775
St Vincent and the Grenadines	115,880	3,007	5,330	80	0.755
Suriname	419,660	1,803	4,599	77	0.762
Swaziland	1,067,940	1,175	4,330	133	0.547
Tonga	100,720	1,371	–	–	–
Trinidad and Tobago	1,309,610	6,983	9,100	54	0.802
Tuvalu	10,000	–	–	–	–
Vanuatu	201,190	1,096	3,190	128	0.568

Source: UNDP, *Human Development Report 2003*; World Bank, *World Development Indicators 2003*

[a]Rank out of 175 countries in Human Development Index.

2
Understanding Competitiveness in a Global World

This chapter sets out the framework and context within which we explore competitiveness in small states. It looks at the importance of knowledge in the new globalised world, and the challenge to small states to harness this. The role of policies and institutions are explored, including the potential for a National Innovation System.

2.1 The Importance of Knowledge in Globalisation

Accelerating globalisation is the international landscape within which strategies for improving competitiveness in small states need to be developed. The process of world economic integration over the last two decades has involved a merging of national markets for goods, services and factors of production (labour, capital and technology) into world markets (see Crafts, 2000; Ghose, 2003; Stiglitz, 2003). The outcome is an international market that seems indifferent to national boarders and state regulation. Globalisation is being driven by powerful factors: falling trade barriers (through the implementation of the Uruguay Round and economic liberalisation), increasing technological advances (for example ICT, biotechnology, robotics and automation technologies), declining communication and transport costs, migration of technical and professional manpower and highly mobile multinational corporations seeking out new investments. The process has profound implications for small states and enterprises within them.

From the viewpoint of small states competitiveness, one feature of globalisation is particularly relevant: knowledge and technological progress have become more important to the realisation of economic prosperity within an integrated world economy (see UNIDO, 2002; ADB, 2003). It should be noted that this is true for all sectors of the economy, and that it applies equally to manufacturing and the services sector. In many small states significant focus has been given to the opportunities that globalisation and the knowledge economy will bring to the services sector, for example the promotion of the idea of back office centres to attract investment in areas such as call centres and data processing. However, globalisation and the knowledge economy is also exerting a profound influence on the behaviour of *manufacturing* enterprises and the environment around them by altering production processes, new product introduction, supply-chain relationships between firms, demand conditions and regulations (Box 2.1).

Box 2.1: The Knowledge-driven Global Economy and Small States

Globalisation is radically altering the nature of industrialisation and enterprises in small states. Knowledge and technological progress have become central to economic prosperity in an integrated world economy. This has led to the term 'knowledge-driven economy' to describe an economy in which the generation and exploitation of knowledge has come to play the predominant part in the creation of wealth. The term refers to the exploitation and use of knowledge in all production and service activities and not just those sometimes classified as high tech or knowledge intensive. Knowledge and technology have always been important but five mutually reinforcing processes are increasing its importance for economic prosperity in small states:

1. *Revolutionary changes in ICT* are transforming every stage of manufacturing (for example finding new technology, management of supply-chain relationships and accessing distant markets) and creating entirely new products (for example digital televisions) and new services such as software services). Enterprises need to develop efficient manufacturing capabilities (via engineering and research and development) to cope with rapid technological progress.

2. The rise of *globally integrated value chains*, driven by multinational corporations (MNCs), are creating 'first mover' advantages for enterprises that manage to insert themselves early into subcontracting relationships. Over time, such enterprises can learn and improve their competitiveness by accessing the new technologies, managerial practices, technical skills and marketing connections of MNCs.

3. *New rules of the game* (introduced through the WTO and by foreign buyers of output) mean that enterprises have to comply with higher technical, environmental and labour standards in export markets such as ISO 9000 and ISO 14000, technical barriers to trade (TBT) and sanitary and phytosanitary measures (SPS).

4. *Changing consumer demand* (associated with rising incomes and changing tastes) for more sophisticated, customised and environmentally friendly products places new demands on enterprises. This means that there is a premium on accessing up-to-date market information and ensuring that production processes and product designs are more flexible and closely adapted to changing markets.

5. *Increasing global competition* associated with falling trade barriers and transport costs require enterprises to add more value in production processes to compete against lower-cost rivals.

These processes are revolutionising the way in which enterprises and governments in small states need to operate. They call for a renewed focus on knowledge as a means of improving firm-level competitiveness and on coherent policies to support industrial restructuring. Close interactions between business associations and governments are also increasingly important to implement a coherent policy framework for competitiveness and to ensure that national obstacles (for example cumbersome bureaucratic procedures and inefficiencies in infrastructure) are swiftly dealt with.

Source: Based on UNIDO (2002)

This new manufacturing context, based on knowledge and technological progress, provides unparalleled new opportunities and poses new risks for enterprises in small states. On the one hand, it has the potential to offer enterprises in small states with access to a virtually unlimited pool of global assets. These assets include not only new markets in both developed and developing countries, but perhaps more importantly resources such as new technologies, information, skills and capital. A lack of resources and small markets at national level will pose less of a constraint to industrial growth and structural transformation as enterprises link up with foreign buyers and multinationals and draw on vast global resources and markets. Hence, the dynamics of globalisation can propel faster industrial growth, exports and greater economic prosperity in small states than ever before.

On the other hand, world economic integration brings about a sudden, marked increase in competition for enterprises in domestic markets – from imports, the entry of new foreign investors and expanding large domestic firms. There is also likely to be more intense competition within the developing world for export markets, foreign investment and resources. Many small states have underestimated the intensity of global competition and its effects on their enterprises. Accordingly, adjusting to increased global competition has placed unprecedented demands on the capacities of enterprises, business associations, support institutions and governments. In general, old structures, institutions, behavioural patterns and public policies seem ill-adapted to deal with the challenge of global competition. There is an imperative to look outside familiar paradigms for innovative policy and enterprise solutions, and to examine how the competitiveness of the system as a whole can be increased.

2.2 Diverse Perspectives on Competitiveness

Competitiveness is regularly mentioned in newspapers and popular discussions of economic issues in small states but a common definition is not used.[3] This makes it difficult to interpret some of the views and proposals. Closer analysis suggests that two distinct perspectives underlie most discussions.[4] Each has a different definition of competitiveness and proposes a different solution.

One is embedded in standard macroeconomic theory and is concerned with simultaneously ensuring internal (i.e. full employment) and external balance (i.e. current account equilibrium) in the short run. This perspective highlights links between changes in the balance of payments, movements in the real exchange rate, shifts in resource allocation between sectors and changes in competitiveness. Emphasising the behaviour of the real exchange rate as the mechanism for adjustment, it implicitly associates it with short-run competitiveness. Hence, a country is deemed to be more competitive if its real exchange rate depreciates and less competitive if it appreciates. Real exchange rate management is widely used by central banks in small states to track short-run competitiveness and make adjustments as required.

A second perspective has micro-level origins and is associated with business and entrepreneurship studies. It seems to reduce competitiveness to a matter of entrepreneurship in the sense of having a sufficient number of individuals with the initiative and discipline to establish and operate a business for exports. This has somewhat broader policy implications than the first perspective. In its simplest version, it holds that entrepreneur-led firms need access to new market information, stable macroeconomic conditions, market-driven signals and the supply of human capital. Some variants of this perspective also emphasise the role of foreign investment in transferring technology and stimulating local entrepreneur-led firms.

> **Box 2.2: Defining Industrial Competitiveness in Small Developing States**
>
> A concise definition of micro- and macro-level competitiveness from a technology and innovation perspective can be found in OECD (1992):
>
> *In microeconomics, competitiveness refers to the capacity of firms to compete, to increase their profits and to grow. It is based on costs and prices, but more vitally on the capacity of firms to use technology and the quality and performance of products. At the macroeconomic level, competitiveness is the ability of a country to make products that meet the test of international competition while expanding domestic real income* (adapted from OECD, 1992:237).
>
> The OECD definition of industrial competitiveness is simple and internally consistent. It highlights the relevance of price and non-price factors at the micro-level and emphasises that technological and marketing considerations are the paramount drivers of enterprise success. It translates these ideas to the national level by suggesting that industrial outputs (i.e. goods and services) have to meet the price, quality and delivery standards of increasingly open, domestic and international markets. This is particularly pertinent in today's progressively integrated world economy with falling trade barriers, accelerating technological progress and increasing MNC activity. The definition also links the performance of a country's industries to rising living standards, thereby adhering to the empirically observed relationship between exports and economic growth. This last point is particularly important for policy purposes and the UK Government White Papers on competitiveness and the US Competitiveness Policy Council have followed the OECD in viewing competitiveness as the ability to raise living standards.

Macroeconomic and entrepreneurship factors are necessary conditions for the competitiveness of small states. Few would be able to create competitiveness without a stable macroeconomic environment and dedicated entrepreneurs. It is increasingly believed, however, that these factors on their own may be insufficient to ensure a continuous process of competitiveness at enterprise level in small states. The recent literature on technological capabilities and the related literature on national innovations systems stresses the difficult firm-specific processes that are involved in building technological and other critical export capabilities (for example marketing and human resources) in developing countries.[5] This approach, termed the technology and innovation perspective on competitiveness, can be readily adapted in this study to the circumstances of small states.

The technology and innovation perspective recognises that small states have access to a global pool of technologies and are typically users of imported technology rather than producers. It focuses on manufacturing enterprises as the main actors in the process of accumulating technological and other export capabilities (for example marketing and human resources). It emphasises the notion that enterprises have to undertake conscious investments to convert imported technologies into productive use. New technologies have a large tacit element (i.e. person-embodied information which is difficult to articulate in hardware or written instructions) that can only be acquired through experience and deliberate investments in training, information search, engineering activities and even research and development. This directly leads to the issue of defining the notion of industrial competitiveness and making the link between the enterprise and national levels (see Box 2.2).

2.3 Enterprise-level Learning and Competitiveness

Figure 2.1 shows a simple representation of the learning process at enterprise level in a typical small state. The diagram links four critical elements of this process: imported technology, firm-level effort, inputs into enterprise learning and phases of technological development.

Starting at the top left of the diagram, enterprises begin by importing technology in embodied forms (foreign direct investment, licensing, equipment and copying). Then they invest in building their abilities to master the tacit elements of the technology. They draw upon a variety of internal inputs (human resources, technological effort, management effort and organisation effort) and external inputs (other firms, technology support, skills, finance and infrastructure) to build up their capabilities. The process starts with capabilities needed to master the technology for production purposes and may deepen over time into improving the technology and creating new technology. These concepts are illustrated in Box 2.3 by examples of learning in African small and medium enterprises in Kenya and Ghana. These examples were selected because of the similarities with enterprises in small states. Kenya and Ghana are not small states. Chapters 4 and 5 on Mauritius and Trinidad and Tobago provide case studies of enterprises in small states.

Figure 2.1: The Enterprise-level Learning Process

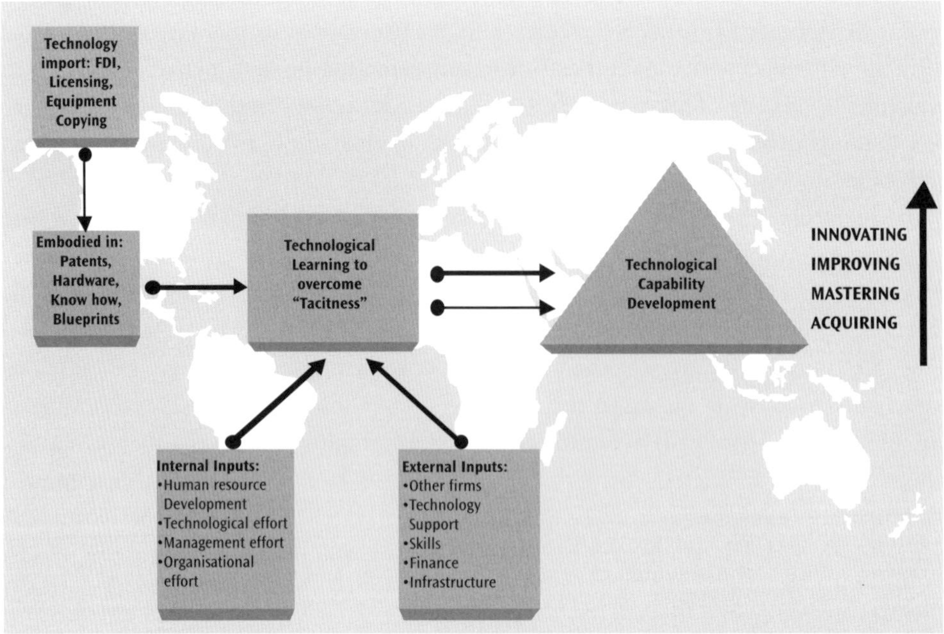

Technology import: FDI, Licensing, Equipment Copying

↓

Embodied in: Patents, Hardware, Know how, Blueprints

→ **Technological Learning to overcome "Tacitness"** → **Technological Capability Development**

INNOVATING
IMPROVING
MASTERING
ACQUIRING

Internal Inputs:
- Human resource Development
- Technological effort
- Management effort
- Organisational effort

External Inputs:
- Other firms
- Technology Support
- Skills
- Finance
- Infrastructure

Box 2.3: Building Competitive Capabilities in African SMEs

Buyer–Seller Relationships for Competitiveness in a Kenyan Garment SME

Bedi Investments Ltd. is unique in Kenya – a local SME which began in the local market and then moved into exports. Bedi was established in 1975 by a Kenyan entrepreneur as a small family-run garment firm, producing for the local market. The entrepreneur was not content with remaining small and localised, and developed a business strategy for Bedi's future growth. Over the years, the firm integrated backwards into making fabrics and yarns and emerged as one of the most modern integrated textile-garment plants in the country. The firm is currently managed by the founder's three sons, all UK engineering or business graduates. The firm has a good base of technical manpower by local standards (2 per cent of employees are engineers and technicians) and by the mid-1990s was spending 1 per cent of sales on training. Bedi gradually moved into exports and was wholly export-oriented by the mid-1990s, exporting goods to the value of US$4 million.

Bedi's move into exports was greatly assisted by a long-term stable marketing arrangement with a foreign buyer. Bedi made contact with the foreign buyer at an overseas trade fair and began exporting on a small scale. The foreign buyer soon became impressed with the price of Bedi's products and their timely delivery and decided to assist with quality improvement. The foreign buyer encouraged the

Box 2.3 (continued)

adoption of ISO 9000, providing Bedi with information about the ISO programme and helping with implementation. Initially, the buyer arranged for an audit by a qualified consultant from abroad and subsidised its cost. It then helped Bedi to implement the post-audit changes in the process, including the purchase of new equipment, metrological tests, training workers and quality personnel, and a detailed monitoring system. Finally it helped Bedi with the process of verification and certification by an independent accredited agency. In 1994, Bedi had a 26-strong quality control department (7.3 per cent of employees) and its internal reject rate was under 1 per cent. The implementation of the ISO 9000 system doubled Bedi's labour productivity growth to 6 per cent per year (between 1984–89 and 1989–94), and enabled it to expand further into exports by attracting two more foreign buyers.

Bedi's technological capabilities have improved significantly over time. It has a good capacity to search and negotiate terms for imported technology; one of the best production capabilities in the Kenyan garment industry (a strong emphasis on quality control and low reject rates, well maintained equipment and negligible equipment breakdown rates, and frequent changes in plant layout); and good technological linkages with foreign buyers and equipment suppliers. However, it lacks independent design capabilities and relies heavily on foreign buyers for product designs. This is a common characteristic of firms in the early stages of export development. The improvement in technological capabilities is due to a strong base of human capital, investment in training, long experience in production and technology transfer from buyers.

Learning to Compete in a Ghanaian Food-processing SME

With 80 staff, Astek Fruit Processing was one of Ghana's leading SMEs in the early-1990s. Using high quality local pineapples, the firm produced an orange pineapple drink as well fresh fruit juices and concentrates on the domestic market. Its volume of sales grew at 15–20 per cent per year between the late 1980s and the early 1990s. In the same period, its capacity utilisation rate doubled to 40 per cent and was expected to reach 80 per cent by the mid-1990s.

The firm made a good initial choice of technology. New equipment was purchased on a turnkey basis from Italy. The Italian equipment was cheaper and more suited to the smaller scale of production of the local market than rival sources of technology. The Italian equipment supplier sent two engineers to Ghana for two weeks to install the equipment and to train the workers. Prior to this, the Ghanaian production manager spent a month at the equipment suppliers' factory in Italy. The two Italians did the layout and provided the necessary engineering services but the Ghanaian production manager and other local technical staff also participated in designing the layout of the plant and positioning and wiring the equipment. Local technical staff worked

Box 2.3 (continued)

alongside foreign engineers in a subsequent investment in a Tetra Pack technology (which sought to substitute paper packing for cans to reduce costs).

Learning about the technology during the start-up and expansion had a significant influence on Astek's acquisition of plant operation capabilities. The firm had a comprehensive quality control system and a laboratory, with trained scientists, that performed checks on the fruit, the process and the final products. The equipment was well maintained by a full-time maintenance team headed by a graduate engineer. Moreover, it developed its main product, the orange pineapple drink, through in-house efforts and experimentation with different formulations.

Two factors underlie the strong local market and technological performance of this SME. It is owned and managed by a highly educated scientist, who has a Ph.D in chemistry from London University and previously worked for the Ghana Standards Board) and his two sons, who have degrees in business studies and mechanical engineering. It has also developed close relationships with technology centres and banks in Ghana and had ready access to technological services and finance.

Source: Bedi – based on Wignaraja and Ikiara, 1999; Astek – based on Lall *et al.*, 1994

Five features of the process of building technological and other export capabilities (for example marketing and human resources) in enterprises in small states are particularly relevant here:[6]

1. *The process of acquiring capabilities is unpredictable.* Investments in capabilities, like financial investments, carry considerable risk and the outcome is uncertain. Firms face technical difficulties and financial uncertainties especially in research activities. Moreover, firms can rarely insure against failure in capability building. The implications of fundamental uncertainty are clear: the reality cannot be fully modelled and the direction of change never achieves equilibrium.

2. *Capability building is an incremental and cumulative process.* Enterprises cannot instantaneously develop the capabilities needed to handle new technologies; nor can they make jumps into completely new areas of competence. Instead, they proceed in an incremental manner building on past investments in technological capabilities and other export capabilities and moving from simple to more complex activities.[7]

3. *Capability building involves close co-operation between organisations.* Small firms rarely acquire capabilities in isolation. When attempting to absorb imported technologies, they interact and exchange technical inputs with other firms (competitors, suppliers

and buyers of output) and support institutions (technology institutions, training bodies and SME service providers) in a national innovation system. Hence, interaction and interdependence between organisations (i.e. collective learning) in a national innovation system is a fundamental characteristic of capability building.

4. *Success in acquiring firm-level capabilities can spill over into comparative advantage and export success.* Differences in the efficiency with which micro-level capabilities in enterprises are created are themselves a major source of differences in comparative advantage between countries. Small states with relatively efficient firm-level learning processes will witness rapid export growth and upgrading while weak learning processes in others will be associated with poor export performance.

5. *Capability building is affected by a host of national policy and institutional factors.* Firm-level learning can be stimulated by the trade, industrial and macroeconomic regime, as well as supported by institutions providing industrial finance, training and information and technological support. In general, macroeconomic stability, outward-oriented trade and investment policies, ample supplies of general and technical manpower, ready access to industrial finance and comprehensive support from technology institutions are conducive to rapid capability building.

2.4 Role of Policies and Institutions

Perhaps the best way to analyse the influences on capability building in firms is to view them as being a part of a system of interconnected elements that are all geared towards collective learning in firms and, hence, attainment of competitiveness. This scheme, termed the national innovation system (NIS) is shown in Figure 2.2.[8] The NIS approach emphasises that innovation and learning are a process that involves more than firms, support institutions, governments and other actors because of synergies and systems effects. It also suggests that the innovation and learning process hinges on the internal interactions between the actors in the system and the external links of the system.

Three levels can be envisaged in a NIS in a small state. The first is made up of the *industrial clusters* within a country. This contains all the firms (producers, buyers and suppliers) engaged in a given industry. In turn, national industrial clusters are linked to various players (for example foreign buyers of output and multinationals) in global industrial clusters (represented by global knowledge in Figure 2.2). As they provide access to imported technologies, skills and international markets, these external links are crucial to local technological development and competitiveness. Of course, links with regional industrial clusters (i.e. regional buyers of output and regionally-based multinational firms) may be more relevant to some small states, particularly micro-states, than global ones.

The second level is the set of *institutions and factor markets* which support learning processes in industrial clusters. There is a strong emphasis on processes of interactive learning, i.e. the exchange of knowledge and information between organisations involved in the development of capabilities. These institutions and factor markets include education, finance, technological support and physical infrastructure. Some small states may rely more on regional institutions and factor markets than national ones. Examples may include airlines and commercial banks based in larger small states which have expanded into the regional market, as well as regional technology institutions and universities which are mandated to service the region.

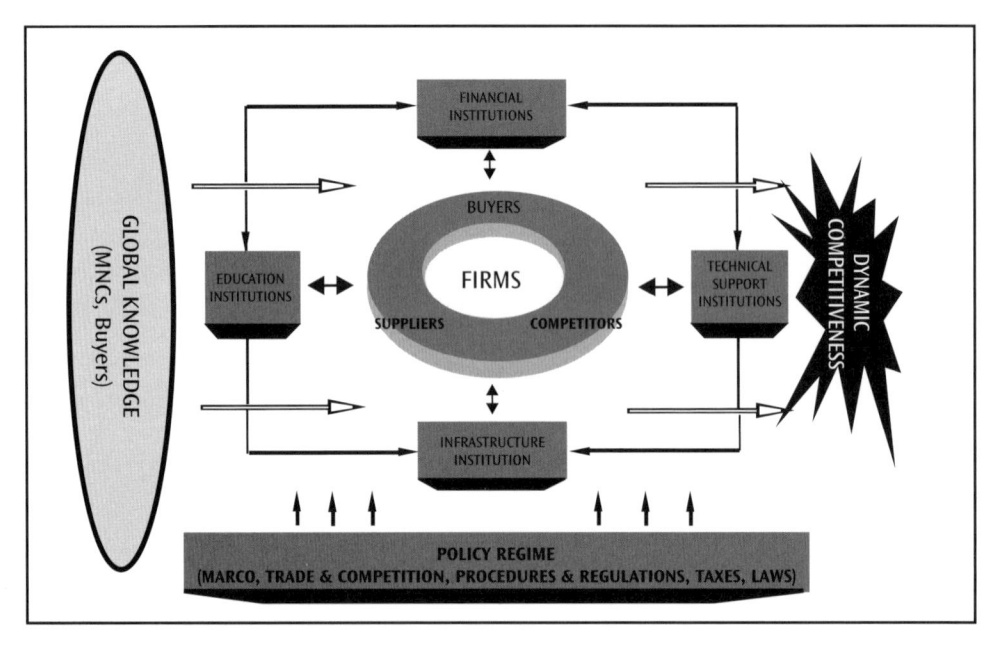

Figure 2.2: National I

The third level is the *set of policies* that stimulate the learning processes between industrial clusters and institutions. A range of policies that influence technological activity fall under this heading, including the political and macroeconomic environment, the trade and competition regime, business and transactions costs, the tax regime and the legal system. Clearly regional trade and investment policies will also influence enterprise learning within given small states.

There are significant differences between national innovation systems across small states due to the following underlying factors:

- The level of technological and other capabilities of enterprises which are contained in industrial clusters;
- The effectiveness of institutions and factor markets which provide education, finance, technological support and physical infrastructure to enterprises;

- The efficiency of collective learning processes involving enterprises and institutions;
- The supportive nature of the policy framework;
- Systems effects;
- The intensity of external links.

Not surprisingly, a few more efficient systems will witness more sustained competitiveness than others. These systems are characterised by a good base of capable firms, efficient institutions, significant collective learning, strong systems effects and well-developed extensive external links with foreign sources of knowledge. Furthermore, efficient systems adopt business-friendly policy frameworks (i.e. those that encourage exposure to competitive pressures and low transactions costs), which stimulate collective learning processes between firms and institutions. Efficient systems witness smoother transitions to higher levels of national capability development from collective acquisition of technologies to collective improvement and eventually to collective innovation. Higher national capability development is in turn associated with better industrialisation, technologically advanced production and competitiveness.

Most NIS in small states, however, are deficient in these aspects and in their competitiveness relative to industrial leaders. Weaknesses in NIS in small states arising from missed markets, deficiencies in key institutions, poor quality and intensity of internal interactions and weak external links are generally referred to as systems failures. Box 2.4 shows a scheme for classifying systems failures for developing countries developed by UNIDO which is also relevant to small states. Since systems failures directly affect how enterprises respond to globalisation, remedying them is the principal aim of a coherent policy framework to promote competitiveness in small states.

> ### Box 2.4: Gaps in NIS in Small States and All Developing Countries
>
> There are pervasive weaknesses in NIS in small states, and developing countries generally, which inhibit collective learning processes and the development of industrial competitiveness. UNIDO (2002) advocates a linking, leveraging and learning (LLL) industrial learning strategy to transform NIS in developing countries and classifies these weaknesses under three broad headings as follows:
>
> 1. Those that relate to the ability of national industries to link with global industrial clusters:
>
> - Firms and clusters may lack strategic intelligence about the organisation and dynamics of global industrial clusters (for example evolution of technologies, markets and MNC behaviour) and are unable to diagnose their relative strengths and weaknesses;

Box 2.4 (continued)

- Business associations and trade promotion organisations may lack information about global industrial clusters and be unable to provide services to forge links with foreign partners;

- Policy-induced barriers (high and variable effective protection and controls on MNCs) or geographical isolation may hamper the entry of foreign partners (foreign buyers and multinationals) and imports.

2. Those that relate to the ability of national industries which are already linked to global industrial clusters to leverage technology from them:

- Firms may not be able to devise favourable contracts with foreign partners, which provide for extensive transfers of technology, skills and marketing expertise;

- Leveraging institutions (such as investment promotion organisations, SME promotion agencies and regional development agencies) may not be able to provide a range of services to firms to leverage resources because they are top-down, bureaucratic and lack technical manpower.

3. Those that relate to the ability of national industries which are already linked to global industrial clusters and leveraging resources to initiate collective learning processes:

- Firms may not be aware of the need for learning and lack basic manufacturing capabilities;

- Producers, suppliers and buyers in an industrial cluster may not connect with each other or form clusters;

- Firms and other actors may be unable to organise collective learning processes to reap systems effects;

- Institutions providing training, technological support, industrial finance and physical infrastructure may be weak or fragmented and unable to provide high quality support services to firms;

- The incentive and regulatory framework may not be conducive to innovation and learning because of residual import protection, overvalued exchange rates, high corporate taxes, poor enforcement of patent laws, excessive rules on MNC operations and weak enforcement of competition laws.

Source: Adapted from UNIDO (2002)

3

Measuring the Performance of Small States

3.1 Introduction

This chapter measures the industrial competitiveness performance of small states in quantitative terms and benchmarks them against each other. Benchmarking exercises of this type allow governments to assess their country's performance in relation to:

- Countries at a similar level of development, or of similar characteristics, which they would like to outperform; and

- Countries at a higher level of development, whose performance they wish to emulate, and whose policy strategies they could learn from in order to do so.

With this in mind, this chapter develops the Small States Manufacturing Export Competitiveness Index to benchmark competitiveness performance across small states. Section 3.2 explores other recent efforts to benchmark competitiveness and highlights the lack of coverage of small economies in these exercises. Section 3.3 attempts to remedy this gap by constructing the SSMECI and presents the results. Section 3.4 provides possible explanations for the competitiveness record in small states through simple statistical analysis of the SSMECI.

3.2 Current Benchmarking Initiatives and Their Appropriateness for Small States

Benchmarking of the type being undertaken here on competitiveness performance across countries has been the focus of increasing interest in recent years. Current benchmarking initiatives include the following:

- The World Economic Forum's (WEF) *Global Competitiveness Report*;

- The International Institute for Management Development's (IMD) *World Competitiveness Yearbook*;

- UNIDO's *World Industrial Development Report*;

- Wignaraja and Taylor (2003).

Table 3.1 summarises the key features of these four initiatives.

Table 3.1: Features of Recent Competitiveness Indices

Publication	World Economic Forum (2003)	Institute of Management Development (2003)	UNIDO (2002)	Wignaraja and Taylor (2003)
Name of index	'Growth Competitiveness Index'	'World Competitiveness Scoreboard'	'Competitiveness Industrial Performance Index'	'Manufactured Export Competitiveness Index'
Concept	Business school approach to measuring national level competitiveness, using both performance and explanatory variables	Business school approach to measuring national level competitiveness, using both performance and explanatory variables	Focused on industrial performance and national ability to produce manufactures competitively	Focused on industrial performance and national ability to produce manufactures competitively
Number of Variables	160	321	4	3
Weighting System	Two tier approach based on a concept of 'core' or 'non-core' innovator countries. Different aggregations and weightings apply to each group in the final index	Twenty categories each weighted at 5 per cent	Four variables, equally weighted	Three variables weighted at 30, 30 and 40 per cent (with technology intensity of exports weighted higher)
Data Source Type	Published data and entrepreneur surveys (7,741 responses)	Published data and entrepreneur surveys (over 4,000 responses)	Published data	Published data
Country coverage (including small states)	Covers 102 countries (eight small states)	Covers 59 countries (no small states)	Covers 87 countries (three small states)	Covers 80 countries (11 small states)
First published/ frequency	Yearly since 1979	Yearly since 1990	2002 and henceforth periodically	2003

The work of the WEF and the IMD, both based in Switzerland, has largely dominated the global competitiveness benchmarking industry. Annual rankings of competitiveness in developed and developing countries have been produced for 24 years by the WEF's *Global Competitiveness Report* and for 13 years by the IMD's *World Competitiveness Yearbook*. Both indices focus on the micro-level business perspective and examine the extent to which nations provide an environment in which enterprises can compete. In line with this, rather than focusing on trying to calculate a measure of *actual* competitive performance, both adopt an approach of looking at a wide range of factors that could *affect* national competitiveness. To this end they use a large basket of variables (160 for WEF and 321 for IMD in 2003), which include both 'hard' published statistics and 'soft' data from surveys of businessmen. The sample size of these surveys is rapidly increasing with 7,741 responses to the WEF 'Executive Opinion Survey' in 2003, compared with 4,600 in 2001.

Both indices are widely used and have attracted considerable attention in the media. They have also generated a wealth of empirical data. So what light can they shed on the competitiveness of small states? Unfortunately, the answer is very little. Despite increasing its coverage from 80 to 102 countries, the WEF index only includes eight countries of the 47 small states in our study. The situation with the IMD index is even worse, with no small states among the 59 countries that it covers. The precise reasons for this lack of coverage are unknown, and without discussion with the institutions involved any attempts to determine such reasons remain simple guesses. However, one of the most significant factors is likely to be that the very complexity of both the indices means that the data requirements simply cannot be met by small states. With small populations and often underdeveloped institutions small states simply do not have the capacity to collect the data required.

The specific issues of small states may also mean that the general theory of competitiveness espoused by both the WEF and IMD is inappropriate for the measurement of competitiveness in the small states context. In small, developing economies, focus on the basic economic fundamentals (macroeconomic stability, outward-oriented trade policies, high levels of human capital and efficient infrastructure) is perhaps more appropriate than worrying about the 200 sub-complexities found in the sophisticated multi-sectoral economies of the developed world.

Quite apart from the lack of attention given to small states, the WEF and IMD competitiveness indices have attracted criticism on technical grounds. Lall (2001b) provides a comprehensive analysis of the WEF index for 2000 and finds flaws in its definition of competitiveness, model specification, choice of variables, identification of casual relations and use of data. He goes on to offer some insights into the construction of competitiveness indices, and although he is not writing with small states in mind, his comments are perhaps particularly relevant in the context of small states:

> To be analytically acceptable, however, all such efforts should be more limited in coverage, focusing on particular sectors rather than economies as a whole and using a smaller number of critical variables rather than putting in everything the economics, management, strategy and other disciplines suggest. They should also be more modest in claiming to quantify competitiveness: the phenomenon is too multifaceted and complex to permit easy measurement.
>
> Lall (2001b), p. 1520

Wignaraja and Taylor (2003) also offer a critique of the theory and methodology used by the WEF and IMD, including a detailed exploration of the IMD index of 2001. In summary they find that the IMD rankings have:

- *An ambiguous theoretical basis:* The theoretical linkages between the input determinants and national competitiveness are weak. The 'fundamentals' of the IMD 2001 index (pp. 43–49), which detail the 'four fundamental forces of competitiveness', are more of a schema than a theory.

- *Problems of index construction:* The justification for the weightings given to each of the indicators is sometimes weak and often non-transparent. There also seems to be a lack of distinction between variables that indicate competitiveness and those that determine it, with both types used. These lead to problems in interpreting the results and in applying lessons to other countries.

- *Ad hoc data and proliferation of components:* The use of survey data can be problematic in that the perceptions of businessmen in one country cannot be directly compared with the views of businessmen in another country without some kind of mediation. The justification for the recent proliferation of indicators is also weak, with no explanation as to what is being gained by adding more indicators.

Building on this critique, and on the argument that such indices need to be less ambitious and analytically simpler, recent work by UNIDO (2002) and Wignaraja and Taylor (2003) has emphasised the industrial competitiveness performance of developing countries.[9] This is a departure from the somewhat broader (and more vague) concept of national competitiveness implicit in the WEF and IMD work. The two new indices were not developed from a small states-specific perspective, but come closer to the methodology appropriate for this study, and the context of data-sparse small states.

The UNIDO Competitive Industrial Performance Index focuses on the national ability to produce manufactures competitively and is constructed from four basic indicators.

- Manufacturing value added (MVA) per capita;
- Manufactured exports per capita;
- Share of medium and high-tech activities in MVA;
- Share of medium and high-tech products in manufactured exports.

The UNIDO index provides valuable insights into the industrial record of the developing world. Unfortunately, of 87 countries listed in the index, only three are small states as defined in our study. Again, the reasons are unclear, but perhaps even such a simplified index still poses data availability problems.

Wignaraja and Taylor use similar analytical underpinning to UNIDO and construct a Manufactured Export Competitiveness Index (MECI) of 80 developing countries using three variables:

- Manufacturing exports per capita (1999);
- Average manufactured export growth per annum (1980–99);
- Technology-intensive exports as percentage of total merchandise exports (1998).[10]

Of the 80 countries in the MECI, 11 are small states. The results for these economies are shown in Table 3.2 below. The top and bottom three results in the overall MECI are also shown in order to give context to the data and index values for small states.

Table 3.2: Summary of Results from MECI

Overall Rank	Country	MECI Index Value	Manufactured Exports per Capita, 1999 (current $US)		Average Manufactured Export Growth % per year (1980–1999)		Technology Intensive Exports (% of Total Merchandise Exports), 1998	
			Rank	Value	Rank	Value	Rank	Value
1	Singapore	0.93	1	25,039	13	13.4	1	70
2	Malaysia	0.82	5	2,988	3	19.2	4	55
3	Taiwan	0.79	3	5,477	31	9.4	3	58
15	Trinidad and Tobago	0.52	16	645	37	7.7	14	23
24	Mauritius	0.45	12	984	15	12.8	43	3
26	Cyprus	0.45	15	684	62	3.1	23	17
30	Bahrain	0.42	13	953	19	11.6	65	0
38	Dominica	0.38	21	393	34	9.2	65	0
45	Jamaica	0.35	22	377	64	2.8	43	3
50	St Kitts and Nevis	0.33	26	300	57	3.8	65	0
55	Grenada	0.31	52	45	42	7.2	65	0
58	Belize	0.29	41	86	69	0.4	49	2
61	Guyana	0.27	53	37	67	0.9	43	3
67	Tonga	0.24	72	6	50	5.9	65	0
78	Congo, DR	0.15	76	1	74	−2.1	58	1
79	Nigeria	0.13	80	1	71	−1.2	58	1
80	Yemen, Republic of	0.00	78	1	80	−18.0	65	0

Source: Wignaraja and Taylor, 2003

The 11 small states are fairly evenly spread through the middle section of the index, but even the highest performers have MECI values substantially below those of the east

Asian tiger economies (such as Singapore, Malaysia and Taiwan) at the top of the rankings, which puts the performance of small states in perspective. One of the reasons for this is perhaps the universally low level of high technology exports in the small states (whether due to lack of productive capacity or lack of data). While the share of high technology exports was an appropriate variable for the study of 80 developing countries, its applicability for work which focuses on small states exclusively is called into question, as it is either unavailable or not distinctive enough among a small states sample.

Significant differences in the performance of individual small states are visible. Trinidad and Tobago, Mauritius and Cyprus stand out among the sample of 11 small states in the MECI rankings. Explanations for the impressive industrial competitiveness record of Trinidad and Tobago and Mauritius are discussed in Chapters 4 and 5 of this study. In contrast, smaller Caribbean economies, such as St Kitts and Nevis, Grenada, Belize and Guyana, and Tonga in the Pacific have performed poorly compared to the three leading small states.

3.3 A Small States Specific Competitiveness Index

Bearing in mind the limited coverage of small states in the mainstream competitiveness literature and the specific issues surrounding measurement of their performance, efforts to benchmark the export performance of small states require a new small states specific index. As many of the existing methodologies are inappropriate for small states, the design of such an index and the interpretation of its results need to be handled with care. Building on the analytical framework for competitiveness in Chapter 2 and the empirical work of Wignaraja and Taylor (2003), a simple, transparent Small State Manufactured Export Competitiveness Index was developed. The key features of this index are highlighted in Box 3.1 while the rest of the section presents the results by country and aggregate categories.

3.3.1 Country-level Findings

Country-level rankings of competitiveness generate considerable interest in academic and policy circles. Of particular interest are the top performers. Before considering the composite SSMECI rankings, it is useful to start with a brief look at the component variables. Table 3.3 shows the top ten performers for each of the three component variables in the SSMECI. It is noticeable that there is considerable difference in the ranking of the three tables, and that top performers in one component are not necessarily top in others. However, some countries rank consistently high, for example Estonia, which ranks third, third and fourth respectively. The Seychelles also figures in all three lists, albeit at the bottom end. Some countries which figure highly in two of the components, such as Mauritius in per capita manufactured exports and manufacturing value added as a percentage of GDP, do not figure well in the third component, average growth, and this ultimately leads to a lower overall ranking in overall SSMECI. At the same time, a

Box 3.1: Small States Manufactured Export Competitiveness Index

The SSMECI emphasises the ability to produce manufactures competitively in the world's smallest economies. It has been designed in light of the problems with data availability in some small states and the need to build in realistic data requirements in order to make the country coverage of the index as wide as possible. The SSMECI is composed of only three variables, each of which captures a different aspect of industrial competitiveness and which combine to create a simple but effective snapshot of the economy's overall international competitiveness in this area. They are:

- Current performance in world export markets scaled by size;
- The dynamism of this performance over time, i.e. growth rates;
- The size of the manufacturing base in the structure of the wider economy.

The first factor captures an economy's actual record of competing in international markets rather than simply its ability to be competitive. The second captures how dynamic this performance is, and whether the economy is on an upward or downward trend. The third looks at more structural issues, recognising that in a small state where economies of scale are such an issue, a larger manufacturing base is likely to reflect an advantage in achieving competitiveness. To reflect these three concepts and in light of the data issues, three specific variables were selected for the small states index:

- Manufactured export value per capita in 2001 (US$);
- Average manufactured export growth per annum 1990–2001;
- Manufacturing value added as a percentage of GDP in 1999.

Using these variables, the SSMECI was constructed for 40 small states in the Commonwealth and IMF-defined sample set. This sample size is sufficient to be representative and to permit basic statistical analysis of determinants. Calculations were performed to give each country a value between 0 and 1 for each of the three variables, and these were then weighted to produce a final index figure for each country, which could then be ranked. Higher values in the SSMECI indicate greater levels of competitiveness, thus for example, Malta, with a SSMECI of 0.72 is perceived to be more competitive than Djibouti with a SSMECI of 0.22 in Table 3.3.

In interpreting the findings, readers should be aware of the sensitivity of results in small states. When the overall production base is so small, the establishment or closure of a single factory can substantially affect the overall figures for that year. The quality/reliability of the data obtained can also often be poor, due to underdeveloped/understaffed statistics institutions in small states. To a degree, such factors may have influenced the overall rankings and led to marginally higher or lower placement than would be expected. This needs to be taken into account when interpreting the results, though it is unlikely to change the basic patterns.

Full details of data sources, definitions, and methodology for constructing the SSMECI are given in Appendix 3.1.

particularly high ranking on a single variable can push up a country on the overall SSMECI rankings. Swaziland, which comes top of share of manufacturing in GDP, is a case in point.[11]

Table 3.3: Country Rankings for the Three Separate Variables

Manufactured Exports per Capita (current $US)			Average Manufactured Export Growth % per year (1990–2001)			Manufacturing Value Added as % of GDP (1999)		
Rank	Country	Value	Rank	Country	Value	Rank	Country	Value
1	Malta	4469	1	Brunei	19.50	1	Swaziland	31.69
2	Botswana	2891	2	Maldives	17.07	2	Mauritius	24.56
3	Estonia	2203	3	Estonia	16.86	3	Namibia	15.45
4	Trinidad & Tobago	1666	4	Lesotho	15.70	4	Estonia	15.43
5	Qatar	1331	5	Trinidad & Tobago	13.25	5	Lesotho	15.13
6	Bahrain	1080	6	Bahamas	12.89	6	Belize	14.81
7	Mauritius	940	7	Fiji Islands	12.75	7	Fiji Islands	14.11
8	Brunei	773	8	Grenada	12.48	8	Jamaica	13.93
9	Cyprus	605	9	Seychelles	11.19	9	Seychelles	13.73
10	Seychelles	576	10	Suriname	10.36	10	Malta	12.03

Source: See Table 3.4 for a full description of sources

Table 3.4 shows the full SSMECI ranking for the 40 small states, with the component indices, the ranking in each individual variable and the underlying data values.

Table 3.4: Overall SSMECI Ranking

Overall Rank	Country	MECI Index Value	Manufactured Exports per Capita, 2001* (current $US)		Average Manufactured Export Growth % (1990–2001)**		Manufacturing Value Added as % of GDP (1999)†	
			Rank	Value	Rank	Value	Rank	Value
1	Malta	0.72	1	4,469	16	5.36	10	12.03
2	Estonia	0.71	3	2,203	3	16.86	4	15.43
3	Swaziland	0.69	17	299	12	7.10	1	31.69
4	Mauritius	0.65	7	940	22	3.14	2	24.56
5	Trinidad & Tobago	0.59	4	1,666	5	13.25	22	7.99
6	Brunei	0.58	8	773	1	19.50	19	8.42
7	Seychelles	0.57	10	576	9	11.19	9	13.73
8	Lesotho	0.56	24	113	4	15.70	5	15.13
9	Botswana	0.55	2	2,891	25	2.25	34	4.97
10	Fiji Islands	0.55	18	266	7	12.75	7	14.11
11	Namibia	0.51	14	398	26	2.15	3	15.45
12	Bahrain	0.51	6	1,080	21	3.25	15	9.88
13	Qatar	0.49	5	1,331	28	1.73	23	7.30
14	Guyana	0.49	19	207	11	10.02	14	10.15
15	Grenada	0.49	16	319	8	12.48	24	7.26
16	Maldives	0.49	23	116	2	17.07	26	6.46

Table 3.4 (continued)

Overall Rank	Country	MECI Index Value	Manufactured Exports per Capita, 2001* (current $US)		Average Manufactured Export Growth % (1990–2001)**		Manufacturing Value Added as % of GDP (1999)†	
			Rank	Value	Rank	Value	Rank	Value
17	St Kitts and Nevis	0.48	11	514	20	3.82	13	10.33
18	Jamaica	0.48	26	105	18	4.51	8	13.93
19	Bahamas	0.47	12	508	6	12.89	38	3.20
20	Barbados	0.46	13	468	23	2.82	16	9.32
21	Belize	0.46	22	122	30	0.00	6	14.81
22	Bhutan	0.46	28	59	14	6.86	11	11.56
23	Cyprus	0.46	9	605	31	−1.68	12	10.54
24	Dominica	0.45	15	357	19	3.94	17	8.48
25	Suriname	0.43	30	21	10	10.36	21	8.12
26	St Vincent/Grenadines	0.41	25	111	17	5.16	25	6.54
27	Gabon	0.39	29	48	13	6.89	32	5.16
28	Solomon Islands	0.39	21	148	27	1.89	33	5.12
29	Samoa	0.37	34	9	15	5.53	28	6.02
30	Vanuatu	0.34	33	9	29	0.53	27	6.35
31	Papua New Guinea	0.32	32	10	33	−5.37	20	8.28
32	Tonga	0.31	35	4	24	2.33	36	3.89
33	St Lucia	0.31	27	83	34	−9.79	29	5.96
34	Cape Verde	0.30	31	21	36	−10.96	18	8.45
35	Antigua and Barbuda	0.27	20	197	37	−13.97	39	2.25
36	São Tomé & Príncipe	0.24	39	0	32	−3.65	35	4.52
37	Djibouti	0.22	37	2	35	−10.90	37	3.60
38	Gambia, The	0.20	36	2	38	−16.74	30	5.60
39	Comoros	0.13	38	1	39	−26.09	31	5.43
40	Kiribati	0.00	40	0	40	−29.07	40	0.99

Source: Data primarily from ITC, using COMTRADE Database, World Bank, *World Development Indicators* (2001, 2002, 2003), and other regional and national sources. See Appendix 3.1 for full details of data sources and methodology.
*In some cases where data from 2001 were not available, 2000 or 1999 data were used. See Appendix 3.1 for full details
**Where data were not available for 1990 or 2001, the nearest available year was used. Growth rates were calculated using a compound method, adjusting for length of time period as appropriate. See Appendix 3.1 for full details.
†Where 1999 data were not available, 1998 or 2000 data were used. See Appendix 3.1 for details.

As might be expected, two European countries, Malta and Estonia, occupy the first two places in the ranking, perhaps reflecting both greater access to markets and the positive effect of sustained competitive pressure from their large European neighbours.[12] The rest of the top ten is made up of some of the traditional small state powerhouses of the various regions, such as Mauritius from the Indian Ocean, Trinidad and Tobago from the Caribbean and Fiji from the Pacific.

The experience of Malta is discussed in Box 3.2

Box 3.2: Some Determinants of Malta's Success

Malta has the highest SSMECI ranking of the 40 small states in this study and it is interesting to highlight aspects of its performance, determinants and public policies. Malta is a small densely populated island in Southern Europe of just over 316 square kilometres with a population of around 400,000 inhabitants. Its GDP for 2003 was estimated to be slightly in excess of US$10,000 per capita and is growing at around 3.4 per cent per annum.

Export-led industry in Malta started to develop in the late 1960s and early 1970s. Until Malta's independence from Britain in 1964, the entire economy revolved around the servicing of the British naval forces based on the island. When the British forces in Malta downsized in the 1950s and 1960s, there was high unemployment and emigration as a result of the very painful restructuring of the economy. It was perhaps these pressures that forced a newly independent Malta to restructure its economy by developing a local manufacturing base, attracting foreign direct investment and encouraging the growth of a vibrant tourism and leisure industry. Significant progress was made in developing the infrastructure required to support manufacturing and tourism. Attractive investment incentives coupled with low wages, attracted significant foreign direct investment.

Trade Policy

Malta, like Trinidad and Tobago and many other small states, initially pursued a protectionist policy based on import substitution. In the 1960s and 1970s the government pursued an import substitution policy which gave indigenous firms an opportunity to benefit from some of the same operating and fiscal incentives accorded to exporting firms, particularly foreign direct investors.

The globalisation of trade and business generally during the last decade saw a multitude of markets reducing tariff and non-tariff barriers and opening up their economies. Malta's insularity, coupled with the micro size of its home market, meant that its only option was to forge even closer relations with the nearest economic block, the European Union.

Greater Access to Markets

Until recently Malta's relations with the EU were governed by Malta's Association Agreement with the European Community which dates back to the early 1970s. By virtue of this agreement, much of what Malta produced was able to enter the EU duty free, provided that certain rules of origin were met. As mentioned above, Malta's high ranking on the SSMECI reflects both access to markets and the positive effect of sustained competitive pressure from its large European neighbours.

As of May 2004, Malta is a full member of the European Union.

Box 3.2 (continued)

Institutional Support

In 2002, three key organisations comprised the institutional support system in Malta:

- The Malta Development Corporation (MDC) – Malta's national agency to promote and attract foreign direct investment. Established in 1967.
- The Malta External Trade Corporation (METCO) – Malta's national trade promotion organisation. Established in 1989.
- The Institute for the Promotion of Small Enterprise (IPSE) – national agency for the promotion of SMEs and industrial restructuring. Established in 1998.

By 2004 these three organisations were amalgamated into a newly established corporation, Malta Enterprise, whose mission is: 'to enable enterprise to maximise Malta's strategic resources and capabilities to successfully compete in uniquely targeted niches'. Malta Enterprise now acts as a national one-stop shop combining trade promotion, investment promotion and enterprise support functions.

The decision to establish Malta Enterprise stems from the government's desire to improve the overall effectiveness of its trade support network, as well as to enhance synergies between the trade, investment and enterprise functions. The establishment of this one-stop shop is thus a strategic response on the part of government to counter ever increasing competition in international markets for both trade and inward investment.

Recent Competitiveness Initiative

As a small state, Malta is a peripheral economy with a high degree of vulnerability, no natural resources (other than its people) and an almost total reliance on international trade for its economic survival.

Malta has a strong industrial sector based primarily on export manufacturing which today accounts for some 70 per cent of GDP, while its export of services, primarily in the form of tourism, accounts for around 30 per cent of GDP. In recent years, there have been significant developments in Malta's potential in three particular services areas: financial and related services (for example back-office services); maritime services (for example ship registration and cruise liners; and distribution and transhipment services (Malta Freeport).

The Government of Malta takes the view that there is untapped potential in these and other service sectors. So far, Malta Enterprise has responded to the needs of a growing number of clients and users by focusing on the services sector. This focus is predicated on the belief that a strategy specifically designed to promote and further develop the services sector is now required. In line with this, the Commonwealth Fund for Technical Co-operation (CFTC) has initiated a strategic programme to assist Malta in improving its competitiveness in the services sector.

> **Box 3.2** (continued)
>
> Because Malta is a small state, the government believes that the planned, structured development of its services sector is a strategic necessity for various reasons. First, it will help reduce Malta's dependence on manufacturing. Second, it will allow Malta to better utilise its highly skilled, trained and multilingual workforce. Third, it will heighten Malta's potential to sell these services on a regional basis and thus strengthen its position as a hub for international business. Fourth, the local value added component in the services sector could be significantly higher than that in manufacturing as most materials, inputs and semi-manufactured goods are imported. Fifth, Malta's increasing standard of living and attendant increases in the cost of labour and other local inputs means that Malta must move away from the more labour-intensive manufacturing industries to activities that are more skilled and knowledge-based.

The performance of the BLNS states that, together with South Africa, make up the Southern African Customs Union (SACU) is also of interest. All four countries score high: Swaziland is third, Lesotho eighth, Botswana ninth and Namibia eleventh. This high performance may again be due in part to proximity to large markets, and the trade and investment stimulus that an agreement such as SACU produces for its 'satellites'.

Some countries do not perform as well as might be expected. For example, Cyprus, ranked 23, did not perform as well as the other European countries in the sample. Whilst it scored fairly high in terms of per capita exports and manufactured value added, manufactured exports have actually fallen over the last ten years, possibly reflecting a fall in comparative competitiveness, and this negative average growth brings down its overall SSMECI score.

3.3.2 Findings by Region, Income Group and Country Size

In an attempt to establish patterns of performance and provide analytical insights, the 40 small states have been grouped into various categories as follows:

- Geographical region to facilitate comparisons across regions;

- Income per head to permit analysis of different income groups;

- Population to enable analysis by country size.

In each case, the group values for each of the three variables have been calculated using weighted averages, which have then been indexed, using the same methodology as before. Simple averages are also shown for each grouping, calculated using average index values for each country in the group.

Table 3.5 aggregates the results according to geography, allowing the regional breakdown of the results to be analysed.

Table 3.5: SSMECI Performance By Region

Rank	Regional Group*	No.	Weighted Average SSMECI**	Simple Average SSMECI	Manufactured Exports per Capita, 2001 (current $US)		Average Manufactured Export Growth % (1990–2001)		Manufacturing Value Added as % of GDP (1999)	
					Rank	Value	Rank	Value	Rank	Value
1	Europe	3	0.79	0.63	1	2,076	3	8.70	2	12.24
2	Africa	12	0.49	0.42	3	602	5	2.74	1	12.86
3	Asia	3	0.45	0.51	5	351	1	16.95	5	8.46
4	Caribbean/ Latin America	13	0.37	0.45	4	481	2	9.84	4	9.04
5	Middle East	2	0.28	0.50	2	1,200	6	2.41	6	8.21
6	Pacific	7	0.14	0.33	6	51	4	5.01	3	9.53

Source: Table 3.4 and author's calculations

*Regional groupings according to World Bank, *World Development Indicators 2002*.
**Group values calculated from weighted components of sub-indices for members of each region. Where original data for manufactured exports for 1990 and 2001 were not available, data for these years have been extrapolated using the average growth rates of that country. SSMECI values have been calculated using sample maximum and minimum levels.

The high performance of the European region is probably to be expected, as discussed above. In comparison, the relatively high performance of the African region is more surprising, and closer inspection shows that there are in fact two tiers of performance within the region. At the top level, the four BLNS countries, Mauritius and the Seychelles are all in the top 11 of the SSMECI rankings. At the other end, a number of African countries, particularly in West Africa, occupy the bottom ten positions. Overall, the contributions of the top tier performers are enough to obtain a high average in comparison to the other regions. Also of note is the particularly poor performance of the Pacific region, which was not strong in any of the three variables and was significantly lower in the SSMECI rankings.[13] Apart from Fiji at tenth place, the other countries of the Pacific were all in the bottom 15.

Table 3.6 shows the performance by income grouping, which reveals some very interesting results. Rather than running from high income down to low income in a linear fashion, the performance of the four groups is more erratic. High-income countries perform only third best out of the four, with the lowest average growth rates in manufacturing exports and the lowest manufacturing value added as a percentage of GDP. They do have the second highest manufactured exports per capita though, which prevents them from being below the low-income countries. This pattern of results could reflect 'mature' economies that have developed a manufacturing export base, as shown in the high per capita figures, but have then diversified their economies into other sectors such as services, particularly financial services and high-end tourism. In such cases, manufacturing exports per capita would still be relatively high, but growth in manufacturing exports would slow, and value added in manufacturing as a share of total GDP would fall.

Table 3.7 shows the SSMECI performance grouped by population size. This distinction is particularly important to capture the record of micro-states compared with larger small states. In the absence of a universally accepted definition of sub-categories by size, the sample was divided into countries with populations under 250,000 (micro-states), between 250,000 and 1 million, and over 1 million.

The striking finding is that the micro-states record a particularly weak competitiveness performance. This suggests that even within the world's smallest economies, country size matters for industrial competitiveness. Perhaps unsurprisingly, the performance of the larger states was better than the two smaller categories, though the magnitude of this is perhaps unexpected. Many factors probably explain the gap in industrial competitiveness performance between larger small states and micro-states. These include the fact that larger small states have somewhat bigger markets than smaller ones; access to a larger pool of technical and managerial skills; being more attractive to inflows of foreign direct investment; being better able to finance costly infrastructure projects (for example setting up a national airline); and, possibly, being less susceptible to natural disasters.

Table 3.6: SSMECI Performance by Income Group

Rank	Income Group*	No.	Weighted Average SSMECI**	Simple Average SSMECI	Manufactured Exports per Capita, 2001 (current $US)		Average Manufactured Export Growth % (1990–2001)		Manufacturing Value Added as % of GDP (1999)	
					Rank	Value	Rank	Value	Rank	Value
1	Upper-middle income	11	0.84	0.52	1	1,520	1	6.23	2	11.06
2	Lower-middle income	14	0.55	0.40	3	193	2	4.93	1	13.98
3	High income	8	0.36	0.50	2	1,308	4	3.80	4	8.49
4	Low income	7	0.13	0.33	4	38	3	4.62	3	9.09

Source: Table 3.4 and author's calculations

*Income groups according to World Bank, *World Development Indicators 2003*. **Group values calculated from weighted components of sub-indices for members of each income group. Where original data for manufactured exports for 1990 and 2001 were not available, data for these years have been extrapolated using average growth rates of that country. SSMECI values were calculated using sample maximum and minimum levels.

Table 3.7: SSMECI Performance by Population Size Group

Rank	Population Group*	No.	Weighted Average SSMECI**	Simple Average SSMECI	Manufactured Exports per Capita, 2001 (current $US)		Average Manufactured Export Growth % (1990–2001)		Manufacturing Value Added as % of GDP (1999)	
					Rank	Value	Rank	Value	Rank	Value
1	More than 1,000,000	11	1.00†	0.52	1	615	1	5.96	1	12.42
2	250,000–1,000,000	16	0.63c	0.45	2	592	2	4.34	2	8.72
3	Less than 250,000	13	0.00†	0.36	3	123	3	0.48	3	8.27

Source: Table 3.4 and author's calculations

*Population groups as per author's definition. **Group values calculated from weighted components of sub-indices for members of each population group. Where original data for manufactured exports for 1990 and 2001 were not available, data for these years have been extrapolated using average growth rates of that country. SSMECI values were calculated using sample maximum and minimum levels. †The extreme range of the weighted average SSMECI index values obtained (1.00 and 0.00) reflects the strength of the correlation. The group with population of over 1,000,000 was ranked first in all three variables, thus achieving an index value of 1.00 for all three variables. When weighted this gives an overall SSMECI of 1.00. For the group with a population under 250,000 the reverse is true, with last place rankings in each variable giving 0.00 index values, and an overall SSMECI of 0.00.

3.3.3 Comparison with Results from Other Indices

As stated above, one of the reasons for developing the SSMECI is the lack of coverage of small states in the existing literature. The IMD index contains none of the small states in the SSMECI, and so comparison of results is not possible. The WEF index, however, has eight common countries and the MECI of Wignaraja and Taylor (2003) has 11 similarities. A comparison of the resulting rankings is given in Table 3.8.

Table 3.8: Comparison of Results from SSMECI, MECI and WEF Indices

Country	SSMECI Ranking	MECI (Wignaraja and Taylor, 2003)	WEF Growth Competitiveness Ranking 2003
Malta	1	–	19
Estonia	2	–	22
Mauritius	4	24	46
Trinidad and Tobago	5	15	49
Botswana	9	–	36
Namibia	11	–	52
Bahrain	12	30	–
Guyana	14	61	–
Grenada	15	55	–
St Kitts and Nevis	17	50	–
Jamaica	18	45	67
Belize	21	58	–
Cyprus	23	26	–
Dominica	24	38	–
Tonga	32	67	–
Gambia, The	38	–	55

Source: WEF (2003) and author's calculations

Only three countries appear in all three indices, and so comparison across them is difficult. However, if the SSMECI is compared individually with each of the other indices in turn, the results, while not identical, show some correlation. Against the WEF, the results are broadly similar, and while Botswana and the Gambia do slightly better in the WEF rankings than in the SSMECI, the rankings are otherwise fairly similar. The correlation with the MECI is, somewhat surprisingly, less strong, with a number of countries having significantly different rankings. However, if these outliers, including Guyana, Cyprus and Dominica, are excluded, the overall pattern of correlation is again visible.

3.4 Explaining Industrial Competitiveness Performance

Ranking inter-country patterns of competitiveness performance is only the first step in analysing competitiveness. A second and more interesting step is to investigate what factors led to high or low performance. What are the determinants of industrial competitiveness in small states and what lessons can be learnt for future policy development?

The framework presented in Chapter 2 suggests that determinants fall into two broad categories:

1. Incentive factors and policies made up of issues like macroeconomic conditions, import liberalisation and domestic regulations;

2. Supply side factors and policies, such as human capital, infrastructure, foreign investment and technology.

The former frames the competitive environment for business and sends the specific price signals for firm-level export activity; the latter provides inputs and support for this process. Successful industrial competitiveness performance is a result of the interaction of these two sets of determinants.

To fully explore these determinants and to answer the policy questions inherent in them, two kinds of statistical testing, a simple t-test and regression analysis, were undertaken. Given the issues of data availability and data quality highlighted above, this is problematic for small states, but the following sections attempt to provide some preliminary analysis.

3.4.1 T-Test and Variables

A two-sample *t*-test of the variable means is a simple but useful test to analyse determinants of competitiveness in small states.[14] It analyses whether the two sample means are equal, and thus whether the two groups are distinct in statistical terms. By using the top 20 and bottom 20 performers in the SSMECI as our two samples we can determine whether the mean for a particular determinant is different in the two groups. If, for example, the mean value for a particular determinant (for example FDI stock) is higher in the top 20 sample to a level that is statistically significant, this would imply that high stocks of foreign investment are associated with high SSMECI performance, which implies that it has an impact on competitiveness.[15]

Tests of this nature were conducted on 25 separate variables to see which factors were statistically significant. Variables were utilised from both the incentive and supply side categories detailed above and were divided into eight sub-categories:

- *Macro-environment*: A stable and predictable macroeconomic environment, characterised by low inflation and interest rates, sustained GDP growth and high levels of saving and investment, is widely accepted as a fundamental condition for business activity. Five variables are used in this category, covering a wide scope of macroeconomic variables.

- *Country size:* Recent literature has shown that country size is inversely correlated with susceptibility to economic, political and environmental risks. Traditional economic theory would also suggest that larger country size may allow greater economies of scale and scope. Population is used as a proxy for country size as this has been shown to have the same result as more complex indices based on variables such as total GNP, population and total arable land.[16]

- *Trade and investment regime:* An open trade and investment regime exposes the business sector to overseas competition, encourages economies of scale through increased market access and facilitates technological transfer. Three proxies of openness are used as well as inward FDI stock.

- *Vulnerability:* 'Vulnerability', whether in the form of susceptibility to natural disasters or over-reliance on one commodity may hamper the competitiveness of economies. Five variables are used to test this hypothesis, including both singular and composite measures of vulnerability.

- *Structural:* The overall structure of economic activity may impact on competitiveness, with a move away from low-value-adding agriculture into manufacturing and services, freeing labour and benefiting the overall competitiveness of the economy. However, at the opposite extreme, a lack of agricultural and mineral activity may prevent exploitation of potential for value-added industries based on natural resources. Two basic measures of economic structure are used.

- *Infrastructure:* Efficient and cost competitive physical infrastructure allows businesses to compete in the global market without constraint and for small states particularly, modern ICT infrastructure creates the possibility of escaping the 'tyranny of distance', and staying abreast of the latest technological innovation and production techniques. Three variables of modern ICT infrastructure are used.

- *Human capital:* A strong base of productive human capital is recognised as being the basis for industrial innovation and competitiveness. Education and training provide productive numerate workers with the skills to compete successfully. Four variables are used covering enrolment rates at different stages of education and adult literacy.

- *'Development':* Whilst not strictly a 'determinant' of competitiveness, a country's level of development would be expected to correlate with its level of competitiveness, even if the direction of causality is complicated. Three variables are used as a proxy for overall 'development'.

3.4.2 The T-Test Results

Table 3.9 shows the results of the *t*-tests on the means of the variables for high performing sample countries (top 20) and the low performers (bottom 20). Data availability determined the sample size for a given *t*-test. In some cases the sample size would ideally be larger, but in all cases it is big enough to have statistical relevance and it is not low by cross-national statistical analysis standards.

Table 3.9: T-Tests to Examine the Significance of Determinants

Determinants	High Performers Top 20		Low Performers Bottom 20		t-stat	Significant at 5% (*also at 1% level)
	Mean	Observations	Mean	Observations		
Macro Fundamentals						
Inflation % (average 1996–2000)[b]	4.4	20	12.0	20	−1.10	
GDP Growth % (average 1990–1999)[b]	5.6	17	3.5	19	1.75	✔
Interest Rate % (1999)[bc]	13.1	17	16.8	15	−1.75	✔
Gross Domestic Saving as % of GDP (1999)[b]	20.8	16	12.8	16	2.14	✔
Gross Capital Formation as % of GDP (1999)[a]	26.4	16	25.9	16	0.15	
Country Size						
Population (2001)[a]	886,869	20	666,785	20	0.73	
Population (excluding PNG)[a]	886,869	20	425,429	19	2.49	✔*
Trade and Investment Regime						
FDI Inward Stock % of GDP (2000)[d]	75.4	18	42.8	18	1.86	✔
Imports as % of GDP (1999)[b]	62.5	20	66.1	20	−0.31	
Exports as % of GDP (1999)[b]	51.4	19	30.9	20	2.10	✔
Imports/Exports as % of GDP (1999)[b]	111.3	20	97.0	20	0.92	
Vulnerability						
Vulnerability to Natural Disasters[e]	127	17	170	20	−0.72	
Composite Vulnerability Index[e]	7.55	17	7.41	20	0.21	
UNCTAD Diversification Index (2000*)[f]	0.77	15	0.69	13	1.97	✔
UNCTAD Concentration Index (2000*)[f]	0.46	16	0.51	14	−0.76	
Number of Commodities Exported (2000*)[f]	81.9	16	25.3	14	3.62	✔*
Structural						
Agriculture Value Added % GDP (1999)[b]	7.9	18	18.4	19	−3.28	✔*
Services Value Added % GDP (1999)[b]	59.4	18	58.9	18	0.09	
Infrastructure						
Telephones/Mobiles per 1000 pop. (2000)[a]	379	20	220	17	1.90	✔
Internet Users (2001)[a]	46,000	20	33,974	19	0.50	
Personal Computers per 1000 pop. (2001)[a]	87.2	17	79.4	16	0.33	
Human Capital						
Adult Literacy as % of population (1999)[a]	88.6	18	71.5	13	3.07	✔*
Secondary Enrolment (2000)[a]	66.2	13	57.8	11	0.90	
Tertiary Enrolment (2000)[a]	14.9	13	11.5	10	0.62	
Development						
GDP per Capita 2001 (current US$)[a]	6,833	20	2,531	20	2.62	✔*
GDP per Capita 2001 (PPP US$)[g]	10,203	20	5,145	18	3.07	✔*
HDI Index Value 2003[g]	0.76	20	0.67	18	2.34	✔

[a]World Bank, *World Development Indicators 2003*; [b]Commonwealth Secretariat, *Small States, Economic Review and Basic Statistics*, Volume 7, 2002; [c]IMF, Various Country Reports; [d]UNCTAD, *World Investment Report 2002*; [e]Atkins and Easter, 2002; [f]UNCTAD, *Handbook of Statistics 2002*; [g]UNDP, *Human Development Report 2003*.

The main findings are as follows:

- *Macro-environment:* The higher performing sample countries had significantly higher average savings ratios and lower interest rates (both at the 5 per cent confidence level). This may suggest that cost and availability of capital is a driver of SSMECI performance. The means of GDP growth of the two samples are statistically different at the 5 per cent level (5.6 per cent compared to 3.5 per cent between 1990–99). Whilst the high performing sample countries do have a lower mean inflation rate, the difference is not statistically significant at the 10 per cent level. Nor was the gross capital formation ratio.

- *Country size:* Using the full dataset the difference in the means of population size for the two samples were not statistically significant. However, if Papua New Guinea is not included in the sample (at 5.25 million, it is something of an outlier in the group), then the means are highly significant to the 1 per cent confidence level. This backs up the theory that size, even within the small states grouping, is a significant factor in SSMECI performance.

- *Trade and investment regime:* The high performing sample countries have significantly greater means for FDI stock (at the 5 per cent confidence level), which would confirm the suggestion that FDI is a driver of competitiveness, through generation of export production and technological transfer. Unsurprisingly, openness as measured by the exports-to-GDP ratio was significant, but imports-to-GDP and the combination of exports and imports-to-GDP were not significant. On the one hand, this is surprising, but perhaps reflects the fact that all small states are by nature fairly reliant on imports, perhaps even more so if they lack competitiveness.

- *Vulnerability:* Some measures of vulnerability showed high levels of significance, particularly those relating to the structure and diversity of production. The number of commodities exported were significant at the 1 per cent level, while the UNCTAD diversification measure was significant at the 5 per cent level. Perhaps surprisingly, the recent attempts to produce vulnerability indices were not significant, with neither the Natural Disasters Vulnerability Index or the Composite Vulnerability Index producing statistically significantly different means across the samples.

- *Structural:* The structural variable showed that high-performing SSMECI countries had a significantly lower mean for the share of agricultural value added in GDP than the lower performing group (at the 1 per cent confidence level). Given the nature of the index this is perhaps not surprising and represents the traditional shift from agricultural production to manufacturing and industry. The share of services value added in GDP was not significant at the 10 per cent level.

- *Infrastructure:* In the area of modern infrastructure the difference in means for telephone connections (fixed lines and mobile) was significant at the 5 per cent level, suggesting that communication and information flow is a factor in competitiveness. The number of internet connections and personal computers was not significant, however; this may be because it is too early for such new technology to be feeding through to the indicators found in the SSMECI.

- *Human capital:* The importance of human capital in determining competitiveness may be suggested by the high significance (at the 1 per cent confidence level) in the difference in means between samples for levels of adult literacy. For both secondary and tertiary level education enrolment rates the higher performing SSMECI countries had greater means than the lower, however this was not statistically significant at the 10 per cent level. This lack of significance may have been affected by poor data availability in these datasets.

- *Development:* As expected, the relationship between overall development and performance in the SSMECI was strong. Both measures of GDP per capita had significantly higher means in the top-performing SSMECI countries (at the 1 per cent confidence level), whilst for the Human Development Index the means were significantly different at the 5 per cent confidence level.

3.4.3 Linear Regression Analysis

Limited linear regression analysis was also undertaken on the whole sample of 40 small states to complement the two-sample *t*-test. Regression analysis is a more powerful method of depicting causality between variables than the *t*-test.[17]

The dependent variable in the linear regression analysis was the SSMECI and there were nine independent variables under seven headings. The independent variables and the results of the linear regression analysis are shown in Table 3.10.

Even though the method of testing is different, the significant determinants are broadly similar using regression analysis, as with the basic t tests above. This would suggest that the determinants identified as being different between the high and low performing groups do have some causal relationship with SSMECI performance.

Three determinants (number of commodities exported, adult literacy and agricultural value added) are significant at the 1 per cent level, and another four at the 5 per cent level (UNCTAD Concentration index, Exports as a percentage of GDP, Telephones per 1000 people, and population). For some determinants the R-squared variable is fairly high, suggesting a good fit with the index considering the nature and number of variables.

More work is needed to more fully explore the causal relationships between the determinants and the SSMECI, using more sophisticated statistical techniques including multiple regression analysis and panel data analysis. However, the limited dataset available on small states has prevented this work from being undertaken at this time. Further work is needed to secure a fuller small states dataset.

Table 3.10: Linear Regression Analysis with Dependent Variable, SSMECI

	Coefficient	t-stat	p-value	R-squared	Significance Rank
Country Size					
Population	0.0000	2.178	0.0358	0.113670	7
Macro Fundamentals					
Average GDP Growth %	0.0091	1.397	0.1709	0.051439	9
Trade & Investment Regime					
FDI Inward Stock % of GDP	0.0008	1.563	0.1273	0.067044	8
Exports as % of GDP	0.0019	2.570	0.0143	0.151446	5
Vulnerability					
UNCTAD Concentration Index	−0.4391	−2.823	0.0087	0.221580	4
Number of Commodities Exported	0.0022	5.460	0.0000	0.515676	1
Structural					
Agriculture Value Added % GDP	−0.0062	−2.966	0.0054	0.200811	3
Infrastructure					
Telephones/Mobiles per 1000 pop	0.0003	2.271	0.0289	0.119509	6
Human Capital					
Adult Literacy as percentage of population	0.0053	3.610	0.0011	0.310094	2

Source: Table 3.9 and data years

Appendix 3.1: Construction of the SSMECI

This appendix covers the technical details of the methodology used to construct the Small States Manufacturing Export Competitiveness Index, together with notes on data sources and definitions.

Data – Definitions and Sources

Definition of 'Manufacturing'

The commonly used international definition of manufacturing is used throughout, which is defined using the Standard International Trade Classification (SITC) codes. The manufacturing sector is represented by the addition of the values for SITC code levels 5, 6, 7 and 8 minus the value of code level 68. The use of such a definition has both benefits and costs, but in light of the data constraints posed by small states, was the only realistic option. In order to put together data for as many countries as possible, a variety of sources had to be used (see below). The use of an international definition made this task more accurate in terms of common definitions across multiple sources, and more realistic as far as availability is concerned.

Ideally, it would have been useful to define manufacturing to include more of the food processing industry, as this is often a large component of small states' export production. However, without access to disaggregated data for each country this was not possible, and in the interests of larger samples, a more standardised definition was more appropriate.

Definition of Small States and Countries

The standard Commonwealth definition of small states has been used throughout this paper and is used here. Using this classification, 32 Commonwealth member countries are small states. They include four countries with small state characteristics despite their larger populations (Papua New Guinea, Swaziland, Lesotho and Namibia). To increase the sample size slightly, the IMF definition of small states was also used; this identifies 43 small states, and when combined with the Commonwealth list, produces a final sample of 47 countries.

Data Sources

As mentioned above, given the difficulties of obtaining data in many small states, a number of sources were used, as detailed in Table A3.1.

For the first two variables the main source was the International Trade Centre (UNCTAD/WTO) with data extracted from the COMTRADE database. This was supplemented using data from the UNCTAD *Handbook of Statistics*, ITC's PC-TAS, and the World Bank *World Development Indicators*. National Sources were used where there were gaps in the data, or to verify erroneous values. In certain circumstances, gaps in data have been estimated using standard imputation techniques with other data from that country.

Indexing Methodology

The SSMECI is a composite index constructed using a methodology similar to that used for the UNDP Human Development Index (HDI).[18]

Table A3.1: Precise Sources of all Data in SSMECI

Country	Manufactured Exports				Manufactured Value Added as % of GDP[f]	
	Year	Source	Year	Source		Year
Antigua and Barbuda	1991*	WTO[a]/ITC	1999	ITC		1999
Bahamas	1995	ITC[b]	2001	ITC		1999[g]
Bahrain	1994	ITC	2001	ITC		1997
Barbados	1990	ITC	2001	ITC		1999
Belize	1992	ITC	2000	ITC		1999
Bhutan	1991	ITC	1999	UNCTAD HOS		1998
Botswana	1991*	ITC/WTO	2001	ITC		1999
Brunei	1990	ITC	1998	ITC		1999[g]
Cape Verde	1995	ITC	2001	ITC		1999
Comoros	1995	ITC	2000	ITC		1999
Cyprus	1990	ITC	2001	ITC		1999[g]
Djibouti	1990	ITC	1995*	UNCTAD/WTO		1999[g]
Dominica	1990	UNCTAD[c]	2001	ITC		1999
Estonia	1995	ITC	2001	ITC		1999
Fiji Islands	1988	ITC	2000	ITC		1999
Gabon	1993	ITC	2000	ITC		1999
Gambia, The	1995	ITC	2000	PCTAS		1999
Grenada	1990	ITC	2001	ITC		1999
Guyana	1991*	FTAA Web[d]	1998	FTAA Web		1999
Jamaica	1990	ITC	2000	ITC		1999
Kiribati	1990	ITC	1999	UNCTAD HOS		1998
Lesotho	1991	NATIONAL[e]	2001	NATIONAL		1999[g]
Maldives	1995	ITC	2001	UNCTAD HOS		1998
Malta	1990	UNCTAD	2001	ITC		1999[g]
Mauritius	1990	ITC	2001	UNCTAD HOS		1999
Namibia	1991	WTO/ITC	2001	ITC		1999
Papua New Guinea	1990	ITC	2000	ITC		1999
Qatar	1990	ITC	2001	ITC		1999[g]
Samoa	1990	ITC	2001*	ITC/WTO		1997
São Tomé & Príncipe	1995*	UNCTAD/WTO	2001*	UNCTAD/WTO		1999
Seychelles	1990	ITC	2001*	WTO-ITC		1999
Solomon Islands	1990	WTO-HDI[e]	2001*	HDI-WTO		1999[g]
St Kitts and Nevis	1988	UNCTAD HOS	2001	ITC		1999
St Lucia	1990	ITC	2001	ITC		1999
St Vincent/Grenadines	1993	ITC	2000	ITC		1999
Suriname	1990	ITC	2000	UNCTAD		1998
Swaziland	1990	WTO-HDI	2001	ITC		1999
Tonga	1991*	ITC/WTO	2000	UNCTAD HOS		1998
Trinidad and Tobago	1990	ITC	2001	ITC		1999
Vanuatu	1990	ITC	2000	UNCTAD HOS		1999[g]

*Imputed from figure for alternative reference year (1990 or 2001), using total export figures from the WTO and using the assumption that the percentage of manufactured exports in total exports stays the same.
[a]World Trade Organisation, *World Trade Statistics 2002*; [b]International Trade Centre using COMTRADE database; [c]United Nations Centre for Trade And Development, *Handbook of Statistics 2003*; [d]Free Trade Agreement of the Americas (FTAA) website; [e]Data from national source, for example Central Bank or Statistical Office; [f]*United Nations Human Development Indicators 2001*; [g]*World Development Indicators 2001* unless otherwise specified.

Indexing the Variables

For each of the three variables an index value was calculated using the following general formula:

$$\text{Index} = \frac{\text{Actual Value} - \text{Minimum Value}}{\text{Maximum Value} - \text{Minimum Value}}$$

A key consideration in such a calculation was determining the minimum and maximum values that were appropriate. In the absence of a theoretical rationale suggesting definite alternatives, the maximum and minimum values in the relevant sample set were used.

For example, value added from manufacturing as a percentage of the GDP of the Fiji Islands was 14.11 per cent in 1999, the sample maximum is 31.69 in Swaziland and the sample minimum 1 per cent in Kiribati. The index for Fiji is therefore:

$$\text{MVA Index} = \frac{14.11 - 1}{31.69 - 1}$$

$$= 0.43$$

This method was used for the manufacturing value added variable, and the growth of manufactured exports variable. However, for the manufactured exports per capita variable the extremely high values of some countries in the sample meant that all except three countries had an index value of below 0.4. This has the effect of introducing a large bias in the overall index in favour of the top three countries. In order to attempt to discount these extreme variables, logarithms were used in the calculations. However, this over-compensated for the bias, and even low performers were attaining index values of above 0.8. In order to even out the effect, an average of the two was used, i.e. the average of the two values produced from using logarithms and from not using them.

Rank correlation calculations were used to measure the effect of the use/non-use of logarithms on the SSMECI order. The rank correlation between the SSMECI based on a logarithmic approach and the 'average' method above is 0.985, while the rank correlation between the SSMECI based on a non-logarithmic approach and the 'average' method above is 0.993. Thus while the average method refines the index, its overall impact is relatively limited.

Weighting the Indices

The three variables were weighted 40%:30%:30%, with manufacturing exports per capita gaining the largest 40 per cent weight. This approach has been adopted, rather than the perhaps more obvious choice of equal thirds, given the particular interest in current performance and the need to account for the varying sizes of the countries involved.

As above, the ranking is robust compared with the use of an equal weighting, with a rank correlation of 0.993 between the results of the two methods.

4

Mauritius

The Mauritius experience of creating industrial competitiveness is analysed in this chapter. It examines initial conditions, industrial achievements, explanations, institutional support for private sector competitiveness, future challenges and, most importantly, lessons for other small states.

4.1 Initial Conditions and Industrial Achievements

There is considerable interest in the Mauritius experience in academic, policy and business circles in small states, as well as in large developing countries.[19] Over the last 30 years, few sub-Saharan African countries have made the transition to the production of manufactures for export, along with high per capita incomes and living standards for their population. Some African economies have begun producing manufactures for export but, sadly, their manufactured export growth rates have rarely been sustained.[20] Furthermore, they have yet to establish a significant international market presence even in a relatively simple, labour-intensive industry like textiles and garments. Mauritius is an exception in that it has turned in an impressive industrial performance. Of a sample of 40 small states, Mauritius is also the fourth best performer in terms of its overall SSMECI ranking (Table 3.5).

Yet a glance at its initial conditions at independence from British rule in the late 1960s indicated that the odds were heavily stacked against it achieving future industrial success. Mauritius was a poor, small developing state back in the 1960s with a dualistic economy consisting of a high productivity sugar plantation economy and a low productivity subsistence agricultural sector. In common with many other small developing states, it had a catalogue of unfavourable initial conditions:

- Economic dependence on a single primary commodity, sugar, and proneness to terms of trade shocks as well as natural disasters such as hurricanes;

- A remote island location in the south-western Indian Ocean, far from major markets and suppliers in the developed world and neighbouring a relatively weak African market and supplier base;

- A very small domestic market of well under 1 million relatively poor people (GDP per capita was $270 in 1970), indicating limited domestic demand;

- An absence of raw materials and other natural resources (such as oil or minerals);

- Limited industrial experience and skills in the private sector outside a few sugar factories;

- A shortage of capital and an absence of financial institutions and intermediaries;

- A multi-ethnic population (Indians, Creoles, French and Chinese) and signs of rising ethnic tensions in an environment of high unemployment and a scramble for jobs.

Table 4.1: Selected Indicators, 1970, and Most Recent Estimates (MRE)

Indicators	1970	MRE
Share of Manufacturing in GDP	11.5%	20.1% (2002)
Share of Manufactured Exports in Total Exports	14.5%	74.8% (2001)
Manufactured Exports per head	$10.4 (1976)	$936.1 (2001)
Total EPZ Firms	85 (1976)	506 (2002)
Total EPZ Employment	17,171 (1976)	87,204 (2002)
GDP per Capita (current US$)	$270	$3,771
Life Expectancy at Birth (years)	62.5	71 (1999)
Population	826,000	1.2 million
Infant Mortality Rate per Thousand	60	19 (1999)
Land Area (sq km)		2,040

Source: African Development Bank, *African Development Report 1996*, Abidjan; Treebhoohun, 2001; IMF, 2002; *Mauritius: Selected Issues and Statistical Appendix*, Africa Department, Central Statistical Office, 2003; *National Accounts Estimates* (2000–2003), Issue No. 418, June 2003, Ministry of Economic Development, Financial Services and Corporate Affairs, Mauritius; Bank of Mauritius (2002), *Annual Report year ended 30 June 2002*

The industrial accomplishments of Mauritius have defied expectations. Table 4.1 provides selected economic indicators for 1970 and 2001/2002 to summarise its remarkable transformation from a mono-crop sugar producer to one of the leading exporters of manufactures in Africa with an emerging services sector. It has built up a significant base of export-related skills, information and institutions far ahead of neighbouring countries in Africa. The share of manufacturing in GDP nearly doubled from 11.5 to 20.1 per cent. The engine of growth was manufactured exports whose share in total exports increased five-fold from 14.5 to 74.8 per cent. By 2001, the country's value of manufactured exports per head ($936) was the highest in Africa. The rapid growth of the textiles and clothing industry underlies much of the dynamism in Mauritian manufactured exports during the last three decades (see Box 4.1). In the sample of 40 small states in this study, Mauritius is one of a handful to have developed a significant, internationally competitive textile and clothing industry. Its textile and clothing industry is perhaps the oldest and most advanced (in terms of types of goods produced) of any among the sample economies.

Box 4.1: The Importance of the Textile and Clothing Industry in Mauritius

In popular discourse the textile and clothing industry is often referred to as a single, homogeneous industry. However, this is an over-simplification and it would be more accurate to view this global industry as a value chain consisting of five main activities:

(a) Treatment of raw materials, i.e. the preparation or production of textile fibres and the manufacture of yarns, for example through spinning;

(b) Production of knitted and woven fabrics (i.e. knitting and weaving);

(c) Finishing activities for various fabrics such as bleaching, printing, dyeing, impregnating, coating, plasticising;

(d) Transformation of fabrics into final goods, including clothing, knitted and woven items, carpets and other textile floor coverings, home textiles (bed linen and curtains) and industrial textiles;

(e) Distribution of final goods, both fabrics and clothing.

Being a relative industrial late-comer, Mauritius does not have a strong presence in all the above activities in the global textile and clothing value chain. Clothing, the technologically simplest activity with low entry barriers, dominates its textile and clothing industry. For instance, in 2002 there were 43 textile firms and 274 clothing firms. The textile firms employed 7,995 workers, while the clothing firms employed 69,982 workers. The textile and clothing industry thus contributed 26.5 per cent of total employment in the Mauritian economy (up from 9.6 per cent in 1980). The textile and clothing industry also contributes significantly to Mauritius's GDP and total exports – 11.3 per cent of GDP and 56 per cent of total exports in 2002. Most of this GDP and export contribution is due to clothing rather than textiles. Textile and clothing exports are highly concentrated in the US and EU markets, with the US accounting for 31 per cent, France for 25 per cent, the United Kingdom for 20 per cent, Germany for 5 per cent and Italy for 5 per cent. Mauritius seems to have established a significant presence in the medium to high-end garment trade. Among other achievements, the country is reputed to be the world's second largest fully fashioned knitwear producer, the third largest exporter of pure new wool products and Europe's fourth largest supplier of T-shirts.

Source: Based on Mauritius Employers Federation (2003)

The creation of an internationally competitive industrial base has been accompanied by an improvement in economic welfare. Spurred by the expansion of manufactured exports, real GDP grew on average by 5.9 per cent compared with 2.4 per cent in Africa between 1973–1999.[21] Furthermore, it achieved relatively high living standards for its population in relation to its per capita income. The life expectancy of an average Mauritian was an impressive 71 years (up from 62.5 years in 1970) and infant mortality rates were 19 per thousand births (down from 60 in 1970). A per capita income of $3,771 places it within the World Bank's category of upper middle-income economies. This performance has led some analysts to describe Mauritius as 'an economic miracle in paradise' (ILO, 1999).

4.2 Explaining Industrial Success

The Mauritian economy is based on three main economic sectors – manufactured exports (primarily textiles and clothing), up-market tourism and sugar. The country is also trying to develop new comparative advantages in services, particularly in offshore financial services and information technology. Only time will tell whether Mauritius will be able to diversify into such services successfully. Its development path in sugar and tourism has been fashioned by factors including its resource endowment, location and policy decisions. The continuation of the sugar quota arrangement with the EU has been a major influence on the sugar industry. Sugar, followed more recently by tourism, laid the foundations for modern Mauritian economic development by providing a surplus for investment, a pool of managerial skills, employment and an international country reputation for producing quality goods and services.[22]

Table 4.2: Inflows of Total FDI in Selected Economies, 1985–95 ($ million and percentage of Gross Domestic Investment)

	Mauritius	Singapore	Taiwan	Malaysia	Sri Lanka
Average annual inflows					
1984–89	16	2239	691	798	36
1990–95	22.5	4785.2	1207	4444.7	128.3
Average annual inflows (percentage of GDI)					
1984–89	4.3	28.3	3.3	8.8	2.3
1990–94	2.5	28.4	3	22.4	4.6

Source: UN World Investment Report, 1996

While the economic contribution of sugar and tourism should not be underestimated, it is widely recognised that FDI in export processing zones has been the major driver of the export-oriented industrialisation of Mauritius (Dubarry, 2001). Foreign investment brought in new capital and access to overseas markets. More importantly perhaps, FDI also resulted in significant technology, skill and information transfers from abroad. Accurate data on FDI inflows into Mauritius in the 1970s is difficult to obtain but information is available for the 1980s and 1990s. According to UNCTAD data, total FDI inflows (including manufacturing) averaged $16 million per year in 1984–89 and increased to an average of $22.5 million in 1990–95 (Table 4.2). In relation to gross domestic investment, Mauritius's reliance on FDI (2.5 per cent in 1990–94) is comparable to Asian economies like Taiwan (3 per cent) and Sri Lanka (4.6 per cent), but less than large investor destinations like Malaysia and Singapore.

The impact of the relatively small inflows of FDI on the growth of the Mauritian EPZs is quite striking in terms of number of firms, employment and exports since the 1970s (Table 4.1). The number of EPZ enterprises increased sixfold from 85 to 506 in 1976–2002 and total employment in EPZs increased from 17,171 to 87,204 during the same period. Furthermore, virtually all the country's manufactured exports came from the EPZs. The textile and garment industry received most of these FDI inflows and its exports grew rapidly (Box 4.1). Hong Kong and French firms were the first overseas investors, and British and German firms followed suit. FDI in the textiles and garments industry in the EPZs had a knock-on effect on domestic investment. Some large local business houses engaged in the sugar and tourism sectors diversified by investing in garment operations. Through international sub-contracting relationships with foreign buyers and some joint ventures with foreign-owned firms, large local firms benefited from technology transfer and access to markets. Large local firms gradually became major exporters of textiles and garments from the EPZs alongside foreign-owned firms.

Several advantages appear to explain why foreign companies invested in Mauritius in the 1970s and 1980s rather than in other locations in Africa. These include:[23]

- *An outward-looking trade and investment strategy.* Mauritius was probably the first African economy to adopt an appropriate development strategy that centred on attracting export-oriented foreign investment. Initiated with the passing of the Export Processing Zone Act in 1970, this strategy emphasised attracting FDI through the establishment of EPZs, duty-free access to raw materials and a package of investment incentives (see Box 4.2). The Mauritius strategy is interesting and offers valuable lessons for other small economies interested in attracting export-oriented FDI.

- *Preferential market access.* Mauritius has been proactive in fostering market access for firms producing in the country. Its links with the EU have been vital to its drive for export-oriented industrialisation over the last 30 years. As a signatory of the Lomé Convention originally launched in 1975 (and its successor, the Cotonou Agreement signed in 2000), it developed preferential trade and aid links with the EU. It has probably been the most successful ACP economy in exploiting these links. Duty and quota-free access to the EU market, coupled with aggressive marketing of this advantage, has attracted EU firms to relocate to Mauritius as well as encouraging Hong Kong firms to use Mauritius as a production base. Estimates by EPZ firms suggest that preferential market access under the Lomé Convention provided a 15–20 per cent cost advantage to firms producing there. Mauritius was also a founding member of

Box 4.2: Mauritius's Outward-looking Trade and Investment Strategy

The outward-looking trade and investment strategy of Mauritius has many interesting features. Unlike many African developing economies, Mauritius did not subscribe to the orthodoxy of inward-oriented, state-dominated development strategies of the 1960s and 1970s that emphasised import substitution coupled with heavy state intervention in the economy. Instead, starting in 1970, Mauritius followed a mixed trade policy of import substitution coupled with export incentives through the EPZs.

These two trade regimes co-existed, influencing enterprises producing for the small home market and those producing for export. Mauritius began trade liberalisation in 1983 as a part of its 1981 structural adjustment loan agreement with the World Bank. Gradual trade liberalisation has resulted in a regime that is much more liberal than in the past and one of the most open in Africa. Quantitative restrictions have been virtually eliminated; there are few import bans and no local content requirements. Nominal tariffs have fallen; the average tariff for manufacturing was about 20 per cent in 2003 compared with 30.1 per cent in 1994 and 86.2 per cent in 1980.

In an attempt to reduce anti-export bias, Mauritius began promoting exports early and has maintained steady support. The Export Processing Zone Act of 1970 put in place a package of incentives which is available to both foreign and local investors. Mauritius's EPZ programme was based on those in East Asia. The main incentives offered are: duty-free access to raw materials for exports; low corporation tax rates (typically 10–15 per cent); no tax on dividends and capital gains; free repatriation of capital, profits and dividends; and permanent residence permits. EPZ incentives are not automatically available to all potential investors. In order to qualify for EPZ incentives, foreign investors are subject to a detailed screening processes by an investment committee. In practice, however, FDI approvals processes are relatively good by African standards and most are approved in a matter of a few weeks. In 1985, a public trade and investment promotion agency, the Mauritius Export Development and Investment Authority (MEDIA) was established to attract FDI, promote exports and manage industrial estates. In 2001, foreign investment promotion became the sole responsibility of a new, powerful Board of Investment (BOI).

Mauritius put in place infrastructure to reduce the capital and operating costs of exporting enterprises by providing developed physical facilities and reasonably efficient infrastructure facilities. The first industrial estate, at Plaine Lauzun, was initiated in 1968. Enterprises are typically scattered throughout the island in small or individual industrial estates. In fact, the whole country serves as an EPZ. Another feature is the mixture of public and private provision of estates since the early 1970s.

The EPZ incentive package, coupled with preferential market access, low-cost literate labour and political stability, have made Mauritius attractive to export-oriented foreign investment. In addition, image building and investor facilitation by MEDIA has helped to translate general investor interest into actual investments in plant and equipment.

the Preferential Trade Area for Eastern and Southern African States (PTA), which transformed itself into COMESA in 1994. This and the Southern African Development Community (SADC) Treaty provide for preferential market access to the African regional market.

- *Availability of cheap, literate, bilingual labour.* Mauritius is justifiably proud of its record on education and in the African context it has a good base of schooling. Through a high level of expenditure on education since independence, it has ensured universal primary education for the whole population and a secondary enrolment rate of about 60 per cent of the relevant age group. The school curriculum is fairly up-to-date, has a reasonable social science and maths content and gives considerable emphasis to languages (both English and French). Sustained investments in primary and secondary education have translated into a literate, trainable and bilingual labour force for the EPZs. Through the Industrial and Vocational Training Board (IVTB), it has also created supplies of vocationally educated manpower (for example plant supervisors, quality management technicians, equipment repair technicians and clothing designers) for the EPZs. The IVTB is discussed in more detail in Section 4.3. High unemployment in the 1970s meant that that wages for shop floor employees and technicians were relatively low. An educated but relatively low cost labour force thus has been a major draw for inward investment into the EPZs.

- *Political stability.* Compared with many other African economies and small states, the country has a political environment that is conducive to foreign investors and their families. There is a virtual absence of civil conflict and violent crime, which is noteworthy for a multi-ethnic society made up of Indians, Chinese, people of French descent and Creoles. Furthermore, there is respect for the rule of law, a reasonably efficient judicial system, strong adherence to democratic traditions and a free press. Added to this is a pleasant expatriate living environment with good housing, schools and leisure facilities. This is one of the country's foremost advantages and means that foreign investors can set up and operate their businesses without worrying about political shocks and the safety of their property or their families.

- *Prudent macroeconomic management.* Mauritius has had a well-managed economy. Fiscal and monetary policy has been carefully used to ensure reasonable macroeconomic stability in terms of low inflation, a competitive real exchange rate, reasonable real interest rates and good future economic growth prospects.[24] This has ensured a stable, predictable policy regime, which is highly conducive to foreign investment and exports.

- *Relatively efficient government.* At a microeconomic level the government is pro-business. Business associations are regularly consulted on economic policy matters and business interests are usually taken into account in shaping policy. Government officials are typically keen to get things done and there is a relatively low level of red tape and corruption. These issues have ensured relatively low transaction costs to business and made Mauritius attractive to FDI.

- *Comprehensive institutional support.* In order to learn and become internationally competitive, foreign and local firms draw on a variety of technical, training, financial, marketing and information sources. Yet another important advantage of Mauritius was the presence of a reasonably comprehensive institutional support system to assist the attainment and improvement of enterprise competitiveness.

4.3 Institutional Support

Five key public institutions comprise the institutional support system of Mauritius. They are the Mauritius Export Development and Investment Authority (MEDIA) which, through attracting foreign investment, provides overseas marketing support and runs industrial estates; the Export Processing Zone Development Authority (EPZDA), which provides consultancy, training and information services for EPZ firms; the Industrial and Vocational Training Board, which provides training services; the Development Bank of Mauritius (DBM), which provides concessionary finance; and the Small and Medium Industry Development Organisation, which provides extension services to SMEs.[25]

Table 4.3 provides the available information on the five public sector institutions which provide services to enterprises (including their objectives, major services, number of staff and budget). The five institutions vary considerably in purpose, age and size, measured by the number of staff and financial resource base:

- In existence since the 1970s, DBM is probably the oldest of the five institutions. MEDIA, founded next, is nearly 15 years old. SMIDO, EPZDA and IVTB are all less than eight years old.

- The Bank of Mauritius regulates the DBM but the other organisations come under the Ministry of Industry and Commerce (MOIC). Functioning under the strategic guidance of the MOIC, the agencies have some autonomy in day-to-day matters.

- Only SMIDO deals exclusively with SMEs and offers information, training and other services. The other four organisations assist both small and large enterprises, and each has a different entry point to service delivery such as consultancy and information for EPZDA; training for IVTB; concessionary finance for DBM; overseas marketing support and industrial estates for MEDIA.

- Of the five institutions, DBM and IVTB are the largest in terms of their financial resource base and employment. SMIDO and EPZDA (similar in terms of employment and financial resources) are the smallest. MEDIA falls in between these extremes.

Table 4.3: Overview of Institutions Supporting Enterprises (MRE)

Institutions	Core Purpose	Major Services	Number of Staff	Financial Resource Base	Date of Establishment
SMIDO	To provide support to small and medium-sized manufacturing enterprises in order to enhance their competitiveness	Entrepreneurship Development Programme; One-Stop Shop; Consultancy; Awards; Documentation Centre; Common Facilities Centre; Training	42	US$0.87 million government grant in 2000–2001	1993
EPZDA	To provide support to all enterprises operating within the Export Processing Zone	Consultancy; Training; Trend Forum; Publications; Information services; Clothing Technology Centre; User Group	31	US$ 0.81 million government grant in 1996/97; Revenue generated: US$0.26 million	1992
MEDIA	To promote exports; To promote foreign direct investment; To develop and operate industrial sites and estates	Trade Information Centre; Buyer/seller meets; Trade fairs; MITEX; Market surveys; Industrial estates	58	US$2.2 million government grant in 1998/99	1985
IVTB	The promotion, development and delivery of training	Training courses; Administration of training levy refund; Technical advice; Library and information services	500+	US$4.1 million government grant in 1998/99	1992
DBM	To provide concessionary finance to small and medium enterprises	Loans; Business advice; Industrial estates	250	Investment portfolio US$97.5 million – no grant	1970s

Source: Author's interviews with the support institutions

MEDIA is the spearhead for investment and export promotion. Its headquarters are in Mauritius but it has global reach through 14 small foreign offices in target investor markets in the US, EU and Africa. Its services include organising participation in trade fairs and textile exhibitions; facilitating contacts with foreign buyers; undertaking marketing surveys; providing trade information; and managing industrial estates. It has a committed staff and management. There is a strong private sector representation on MEDIA's board (50 per cent) and many of its professional staff have degrees from foreign universities and regularly go on overseas training courses. In 2001, the investment promotion function of MEDIA was removed and vested in a new and powerful Board of Investment (BOI). With 40 staff and an initial budget of $1.6 million, the BOI has been tasked with developing a more targeted approach to foreign investment promotion. MEDIA became the Mauritius Industrial Development Agency and was mandated to provide export marketing assistance for SMEs and to work closely with SMIDO on SME development.

EPZDA's mandate is to improve the competitiveness of EPZ enterprises. As its principal focus is on the smaller exporter, its target population overlaps with that of SMIDO. Given the concentrated nature of the industrial export structure in Mauritius, most of the firms registered with EPZDA are in the textile and garment industry and, in response to their needs, EPZDA has developed a comprehensive range of support services for this industry, for example customised consultancy services for individual firms, a clothing technology centre, technical workshops on garment manufacturing, publications, and exhibitions and trade fairs.

IVTB provides vocational training courses to complement the training services of SMIDO and EPZDA in relation to SMEs. The training levy imposed on all enterprises links IVTB to other SME support institutions. Within this scheme, enterprises are required to contribute a percentage of their wage costs to a centralised fund. When an enterprise sends an employee on an approved vocational training course, it can claim a part refund of the course fee from the training levy fund. Approved training courses are run both by the IVTB (which has vocational training centres covering footwear and leather, jewellery, textiles, IT and printing) and private sector training institutions. IVTB also provides a library and some customised in-plant training services.

The aim of the state-owned DBM is to provide concessionary finance and business advice to local enterprises, particularly small businesses, which find it difficult to access formal sources of industrial finance such as commercial banks. Interest rates charged on DBM loans to SMEs are typically 2–3 per cent less than that charged by commercial banks and repayment periods are somewhat longer.

SMIDO is mandated to provide extension services to local firms that are engaged in manufacturing and that use production equipment that does not exceed 10 million Mauritian Rupees (1993). SMEs need to register with SMIDO in order to access its support services. Registration with SMIDO also triggers exemption from payment of duties on imported production equipment. In the main, SMIDO provides training on small business start-up to new entrepreneurs, training on management and technical topics, the use of a relatively well-equipped workshop with trained staff, access to a documentation centre, award schemes for achievements in technology and exports and a match-making service to source external consultants for SMEs.

It is difficult to evaluate the effectiveness of this institutional support system and to gauge its specific contribution to Mauritian competitiveness. Some impressions, however, were gathered from our interviews with support institutions and enterprises. Our interviews with the above institutions suggested that there were positive attributes to the institutional support system as a whole. In the main, dedicated professionals with a reasonable level of equipment and other facilities staffed these institutions. Moreover, energetic and experienced directors led them. They also seemed to have coherent corporate strategies and implementation plans. Furthermore, our interviews with enterprises and business associations suggested that there was a high level of awareness about the institutions and the range of services they provided. There also seemed to be a reasonable take-up rate of support services by enterprises and the quality of support services was recognised as being of reasonable quality and fairly well delivered. Thus, we can conclude that Mauritius has a useful institutional support system, by African standards, and that this has contributed to the attainment of competitiveness by its enterprises.

4.4 Structural Constraints and Upgrading

In time, however, this early export success via the EPZ ran into structural constraints. From the late 1980s onwards, a significant erosion occurred in the country's locational advantages for FDI and its competitiveness. In particular:

- Labour costs rose significantly, labour productivity declined and absenteeism rates increased;[26]

- The gradual elimination of preferential access to the European and US markets seemed imminent with the expiry of the Lomé Agreement and the Multi-Fibre Arrangement for textiles;

- Residual bureaucratic procedures (particularly on FDI approvals, work permits for expatriate staff and customs) were perceived to be a significant barrier to increased inward investment, which was increasingly focusing on low transactions cost environments;

- There was a marked increased in competition from lower cost producers in Africa and Asia which had liberalised their entry regulations for FDI and established EPZs;

- Inflation had begun to rise and with it came relatively high real interest rates and a tendency for real exchange rate appreciation.

The consequence of these structural constraints on FDI inflows in Mauritian EPZs is clearly visible. Figure 4.1 provides Bank of Mauritius data on actual FDI inflows into the manufacturing sector (i.e. the EPZ sector) in Mauritius between 1985–2002. The data show that annual average FDI inflows declined from $12.8 million per year in 1985–89 to only $4.2 million in 1990–2002. Some leading Hong Kong and French investors in textiles had begun to switch out of Mauritius to other low cost locations like China, Sri Lanka and Bangladesh. In Africa, Madagascar has been a particular beneficiary of Mauritian outward investment (due to its cheap labour and preferential market access to Europe). By 2002/2003, about 40 Mauritius-based enterprises had relocated to Madagascar to undertake textile and garment production for export.

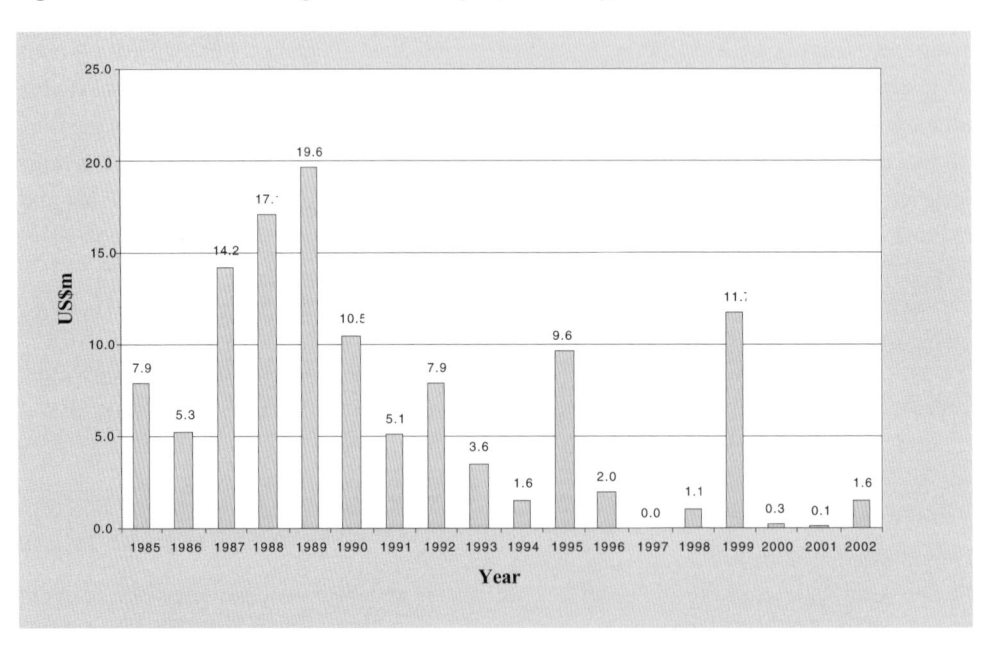

Figure 4.1: Manufacturing FDI Inflows (US$ million), 1985–2002

Year	US$m
1985	7.9
1986	5.3
1987	14.2
1988	17.1
1989	19.6
1990	10.5
1991	5.1
1992	7.9
1993	3.6
1994	1.6
1995	9.6
1996	2.0
1997	0.0
1998	1.1
1999	11.7
2000	0.3
2001	0.1
2002	1.6

It is possible that inherent vulnerabilities associated with the country's small size may have caused the structural problems mentioned above to occur more rapidly than in larger states. Mauritius had a limited base of unskilled labour and technical skills due to its small population. Once the available supply of surplus labour and skills were absorbed in the EPZ sector, wages rose and the growth process faltered. The absence of a domestic market hindered domestic-market seeking MNCs and caused others to exit prematurely. It was at a disadvantage, compared to large economies, in accessing international financial markets and concessionary finance due a lack of creditworthiness to finance technological and skill upgrading.

All of this is reflected in a slowdown in the export growth of manufactures in the 1990s. Table 4.4 provides data on manufactured export growth by sub-periods. It shows that manufactured exports grew rapidly in 1980–85 and accelerated in 1985–92. However, there was a sharp drop in growth rates in 1992–95 and 1996–2002. Some of the smaller exports fell sharply and there was a significant slowing down of clothing exports. Clothing has continued to dominate exports, accounting for 80.2 per cent of manufactured exports in 2002. The slowdown in export growth has had an adverse impact on GDP growth, which fell from 6.2 per cent per year in the 1980s to 4.9 per cent in the 1990s.

There are two other weaknesses in Mauritius's export performance. First, a heavy dependence on a few labour-intensive export products renders the country vulnerable to unfavourable national and international developments in those activities. Compared to other developing economies, Mauritius is exceptionally vulnerable with its high dependence on one item (clothing) that has not declined over time.

Second is the virtual absence of more complex industrial products, either sophisticated consumer or producer goods. Mauritius has 'missed the boat' on the semi-conductor assembly boom that drove the growth of Singapore and, later, Malaysia and produced a variety of related electronic and electrical exports. The lack of upgrading is a significant weakness – it hinders technological spillovers and externalities from complex industries and the creation of new employment in technology-intensive industries.

Table 4.4: Manufactured Export Growth, 1980–2002 (annual average percentage per year)

Product	Annual Average Growth Rates (%)				Manufactured Exports (US$m)
	1980–85	1985–92	1992–96	1996–2002	2002
Fish and preparations	–	–	21.0	10.6	73.4
Pearls, precious stones	7.0	15.3	6.0	4.7	37.3
Textile yarn, fabrics	–	30.9	24.1	–9.4	44.6
Clothing, accessories*	16.4	23.5	7.2	0.5	931.6
Toys, sporting goods	–	–	0.3	–7.4	6.8
Gold, jewellery	9.2	34.1	–14.4	12.0	31.4
Optical instruments	–	–	–	–11.7	5.6
Watches, clocks	34.2	15.0	–3.5	–10.1	12.0
Other**	–	–	–42.4 (a)	–	17.7
Total	16.9	24.3	8.6	0.7	1160.1

Source: Estimated from Bank of Mauritius database
*1992–95.
**Includes chemicals and machinery.

4.5 Recent Competitiveness Initiatives

Having successfully become an exporter of textiles and garments, Mauritius faces the challenge of how to sustain its export growth into the twenty-first century and to broaden and upgrade its base of competitive advantage to cope effectively with different aspects of rapid globalisation, including falling trade barriers, footloose foreign direct investment, rapid technological change and more intense competition from low labour cost producers. In order to respond to these challenges, the government of Mauritius has taken a number of steps to attempt to diversify its export base and to upgrade its competitiveness since the 1990s. Some of the main policy initiatives undertaken include:

- Upgrading the quality and technology of textiles and garments, its dominant export, and attempts to develop new export niches in printing and publishing, information technology services, consultancy services and offshore financial services;

- The establishment of a Mauritius Competitiveness and Productivity Council, with private sector participation, to guide the development of a national competitiveness strategy and to improve firm-level productivity;

- Creation of a new specialised Board of Investment for an aggressive investment promotion drive which emphasises targeting selected activities and investors, cuts approval times for foreign investors and provides high quality post-approval investor services;

- Streamlining bureaucratic procedures for exporters, particularly in relation to customs procedures for imports and exports, procedures for new business start-up and foreign investment approvals;

- Improvements in human resources through the creation of a new Mauritius Institute for Technology to train tertiary-level technical manpower for new export industries and measures to encourage greater enterprise training via tax incentives and worker training programmes;

- Encouragement of enhanced technological activity in Mauritian firms by a public awareness campaign on productivity and quality management, as well as tax incentives for research and development;

- A greater focus on improving SME export capabilities by a significant increase in the operational budget of the main SME extension services organisation, SMIDO, and mandating the restructured MEDIA to provide greater overseas marketing assistance for SME exports;

- Privatisation of Mauritius Telecom in order to reduce telecom call charges, and other measures to boost the development of the IT sector in Mauritius;

- More timely and aggressive exchange rate management to provide a stable competitive real exchange rate for exporters.

Mauritius is likely to face many difficulties in attempting to upgrade its export competitiveness. Groups which have been negatively affected by the exit of foreign enterprises are likely to pressure for protection and subsidies. External shocks (such as a contraction in overseas demand) are likely to dampen export growth. But on the positive side, Mauritius has recognised the urgent need to upgrade competitiveness, to attract more inward investment and to re-engineer its skills base. Moreover, it has actively sought technical advice from abroad, attempted to develop a consultative process with the main social partners (the government, the private sector and the trade unions) and established a strong institutional capacity to implement policy changes. These bold actions increase its chances of success.

4.6 Lessons from Mauritius

What lessons can be drawn from the Mauritius competitiveness experience for other small states? The following are probably the most important:

- Small states can develop export competitiveness and mitigate the economic vulnerabilities associated with small country size.

- Competitiveness at firm level in small states is closely linked to shifts in comparative advantage and needs to be carefully monitored by the government and the private sector.

- The creation of competitiveness in a single productive sector (such as textiles and garments in Mauritius) can bring significant welfare gains to the population of a small state.

- Export-oriented FDI is a powerful means to facilitating the entry of small states into export markets and creating competitiveness.

- A coherent competitiveness strategy is a necessary condition for the creation and improvement of enterprise competitiveness in small states.

- Many policies constitute a coherent competitiveness strategy for a small state. The main elements are an outward-oriented trade and investment strategy; active efforts to negotiate and maintain preferential market access; prudent macroeconomic management; investments in education and training at all levels; establishment of a comprehensive system of institutional support; and investments in physical infrastructure.

- Political stability and close involvement of the private sector in policy-making are also a vital part of a national policy programme to improve competitiveness.

5
Trinidad and Tobago

The experience of Trinidad and Tobago is analysed in this chapter using a similar approach to that used for Mauritius. The chapter examines initial conditions and industrial achievements, enterprise cases, policy and institutional factors and, again most importantly, lessons for other small states.

5.1 Initial Conditions and Industrial Achievements

Just as Mauritius is often cited as the leading success story in the African context, so Trinidad and Tobago is today the most industrialised of the Caribbean small states, and the highest ranking in the SSMECI index in the region. To a large degree this reflects its natural resources and the large oil and natural gas industries that have developed from them. For this reason, the case of Trinidad and Tobago is at first sight less relevant to other small states than that of Mauritius – if a country is not endowed with a resource such as oil, barring a shock discovery this will not change. However, while only a few of the small states in our study have petroleum resources, many countries have natural resources of a different but potentially significant nature. All small states can from the Trinidad and Tobago experience of providing the policy environment to support competitive growth, managing natural resources well (whether they are petroleum based or not) and leveraging from this to diversify the industrial base. Trinidad and Tobago also has success stories in the non-oil sector and is an exception worthy of closer attention.

The initial conditions of Trinidad and Tobago were in many ways favourable, and ever since oil was discovered in the nineteenth century, the country was set on a *potentially* higher development path than many other countries, particularly small states. While the oil industry only really got off the ground after 1910, by the mid-1930s the country had become the leading oil producer in the British Empire. However, as in many countries that have experienced the so called 'curse' of oil, this success led to a comparative neglect of other sectors of the economy, and agriculture and manufacturing suffered a sharp decline.

Upon independence in 1962 Trinidad and Tobago was heavily dependent on the oil sector, and as a result the wider economy, particularly tradable manufactures, suffered from higher wage rates and unfavourable real exchange rates. Coupled with this, the country also suffered from the constraints faced by other small states, such as a small domestic market and limited human resource pool. As such, apart from the successful oil industry, the rest of the economy was weak and relatively uncompetitive.

In the decade 1973–1983, world oil prices rose dramatically and the focus on oil led to rapid growth, with rising incomes, consumption and investment. However, falling oil prices thereafter exposed the over-reliance on oil[27] and led to contracting output, declining per capita income, high unemployment, rising exchange rates and loss of foreign exchange reserves. With little else to rely upon for foreign exchange, the current account went into large deficit, reaching −8.59 per cent of GDP in 1986. In response to this in 1988 Trinidad and Tobago introduced a programme of structural reform and liberalisation, aimed particularly at restoring external balance. Reforms continued in the early 1990s, with reductions in import duties and encouragement of the role of the private sector. As the reforms took effect, the economy rebounded and the manufacturing sector improved significantly. As a result of this resurgence and increased oil prices, the current account came back into balance, and while it is still subject to swings in the oil price, in 2001 it was positive at 4.5 per cent of GDP.

Table 5.1 sets out some comparative statistics for the period just before structural adjustment and the most recent estimates. National income, measured by real GDP,[28] has increased from US$4,940 million in 1988 to US$7,205 million in 2002, while real GDP per capita rose from US$4,096 in 1988 to US$5,466 in 2002. While the manufacturing sector has not grown any faster than other areas of the economy (as reflected in the constant 8 per cent share of manufacturing value added in GDP for both years), its share in total exports has dramatically increased from 23.4 per cent in 1987 to 42.6 per cent in 2001. Accordingly, manufactured exports per head in current $US have increased from US$386 to US$1,655 in the period 1988–2001.

Table 5.1: Comparative Statistics for Trinidad and Tobago – Before Structural Adjustment and Most Recent Estimates

Indicator	Base Year 1988	Actual Year	Most Recent Estimate	Actual Year
Gross Domestic Product (current US$000)	4,496,702	1988[b]	9,400,000	2002[a]
Gross Domestic Product (constant 1995 US$000)	4,940,584	1988[a]	7,205,590	2002[a]
GDP per Capita (current PPP US$)	5,828	1988[a]	9,114	2002[a]
GDP per Capita (constant 1995 US$000)	4,096	1988[a]	5,466	2002[a]
Manufacturing Value Added as % of GDP	8	1987[c]	8	2001[c]
Manufactured Exports (current US$000)	461,300	1988[c]	2,182,265	2001[c]
Share of Manufactured Exports in Total Goods Exports	23.4	1987[c]	42.6	2001[c]
Manufactured Exports per Head (current US$)	382	1988[d]	1,655	2001[d]
Openness (Import and Exports as % of GDP)	66	1987[b]	93	2001[a]
Current Account Balance (% of GDP)	−8.59	1986[b]	4.5	2001[e]
Life Expectancy at Birth	70	1987[b]	72	2002[a]
Population	1,206,310	1988[b]	1,318,300	2002[a]
Infant Mortality Rate	22	1987[b]	17	2001[a]
Land Area	5,130	1988[b]	5,130	2002[a]

Source: Author's compilation based on data from UNCTAD, *Handbook of Statistics 2002* and Central Bank of Trinidad and Tobago, *Annual Economic Survey 2002*
[a]*World Development Indicators 2003*; [b]*World Development Indicators 2001*; [c]UNCTAD, *Online Handbook of Statistics 2002*; [d]Author's calculation; [e]Central Bank of Trinidad and Tobago, *Annual Economic Survey 2002*.

Table 5.1 shows the comparative success that Trinidad and Tobago has enjoyed over the last 15 years or so compared with its own earlier position. The SSMECI developed in Chapter 3, where it is placed fifth out of the 40 countries in the sample, demonstrates its success compared to other small states.

5.2 Selected Enterprise Cases

The success of Trinidad and Tobago in the last 15 years and its rise to manufacturing competitiveness is amply demonstrated by two enterprise-level case studies. These show how firms have used a technological and knowledge-based approach to manufacturing, as described in Chapter 2, supported by the new policy environment and links to the regional market, to achieve significant growth. To demonstrate that this success is not just in the petroleum sector, both case studies are taken from the beverages sector.

The first case study is that of S.M. Jaleel & Co., a soft drinks manufacturer (Box 5.1).

Box 5.1: Strategy, Technical Innovation and Training the Key To Success – Soft Drinks Company S.M. Jaleel & Co.

S.M. Jaleel, based in Trinidad, is a family-run business that is now the largest soft drinks manufacturer in the Caribbean. Dominating the CARICOM market, with leading brands in four different sectors, it employs over 1,200 people in various factories and distribution points throughout the region. Using this base and franchised factories overseas, it exports to 60 countries worldwide and is established in major markets such as the US, where in 2003 it sold 6 million cases of drinks through the supermarket chain Walmart.

This success comes from humble beginnings as a small family-run enterprise which, despite an 80-year history, has in effect been built from scratch in the last 25 years. Established in 1924 by S.M. Jaleel, it enjoyed some early success in Trinidad and Tobago, but as the founder grew old, competition increased and equipment became obsolete it went into decline. By 1970 it accounted for only 1 per cent of the local drinks market. However, in 1980, the founder's grandson, Aleem Mohammed, took over, and transformed it into the successful company it is today.

The reasons for this success are both complex and numerous. Four key factors can be identified which provide lessons to other firms both within Trinidad and Tobago and in other small states.

Technological Innovation: Since 1980 the installation of modern technology has been a key strategy, and large investments have been made in new plant machinery. With a mixture of finance provided by a personal mortgage and seed capital from the Development Finance Corporation, a modern factory was built in 1981, and the company continues updating its technology, currently spending US$3–5 million on capital investment each year. Today it has a truly first world, state-of-the-art integrated production process based on P.E.T. bottling machinery and capable of producing up to 40,000 bottles an hour. It has even been instrumental in the design of new production processes, introducing a new lightweight 250ml PET bottle that is now patented in 150 countries. As a result, it is now transferring operating knowledge back to its US and European partners and earning royalties. The low marginal costs that such a modern production line creates not only keeps S. M. Jaleel products competitive, but has also led to contracts to supply P.E.T. bottles to other firms and to package bottles for other international brands.

Strong Entrepreneurial Leadership: This success has owed much to the strong entrepreneurial drive and leadership of the current chairman. Originally trained as a medical doctor, he devoted years of personal study in order to make the transition to a manufacturing businessman, reading management books and reports late into the night. His desire and commitment to succeed, in co-operation with others rather than at the expense of others, is evident in the company's ethos and working practices.

Investment in People: The company places great emphasis on its staff and invests a significant amount in training each year – 2–3 per cent of turnover. Every worker, of whatever grade, enrols on a structured training programme over three years, which uses a combination of classroom and on-the-job training. This is made up of various modules, as appropriate to the position, with the worker receiving printed manuals and operating procedures for future reference. A recent strategic partnership with the University of the West Indies and the Institute of Business is intended to further develop specific training at higher levels. This investment has paid off, with increasing labour productivity and high staff retention rates – 90 per cent of staff have been at the company for over five years.

Product Development and Marketing Strategy: Strategic thinking has been a key feature behind the success, both in terms of the products developed, and how and where they are marketed.

Product Development – It was quickly realised that Cola was a saturated market, so unique products have been developed, utilising the strengths of the Caribbean, and targeted at specific age groups and sectors. New products have been complemented with innovative bottling techniques, further increasing product differentiation.

Export Strategy – The strategy for developing exports has been based on consolidation, following an 'onion ring' concept. First success in the Trinidad and Tobago market was achieved, followed by success in the Caribbean market, which was then followed by success in the Americas. The next planned steps are to focus on Europe, then the Middle East and Far East. To achieve these aims, strategic use has been made of trade agreements such as CARICOM and of innovative franchising with foreign partners.

Another success story is that of Angostura Bitters, a spirits company based in Trinidad, but operating on a global level (Box 5.2).

> ### Box 5.2: Trinidad's Own Multinational – Angostura
>
> Angostura, an alcoholic beverage company based in Trinidad and Tobago, has a history going back to 1824, when it started producing the unique and now famous Angostura Aromatic Bitters. From this niche it has diversified through company acquisition and developed into a worldwide group of companies, which produces rum, whisky, cognac and vodka as well as the original bitters. Now trading as CL World Brands PLC, it exports 85 per cent of production, has 2,500 employees and a turnover of US$400 million. Thus it is Trinidad's own multinational.
>
> **Balancing Risk with Consolidation**
> Angostura's success has been based on a careful balance of risk and consolidation. The company has been forward looking and adventurous, especially in recent years, At each stage, however, it has taken a step-by-step approach, and has never risked the core business. It has utilised local knowledge where appropriate, but has not been afraid to go global where necessary, especially in terms of technology and marketing.
>
> **Leveraging off a Consolidated Niche and Preferential Trade Agreements**
> The success of Angostura is ultimately based on its bitters, which has a worldwide reputation, and has the history of its secret formula as its competitive advantage. However, as with any true niche market, production of bitters is subject to a ceiling on sales and in order to grow further Angostura have had to diversify. This has been done through clever use of the Angostura brand's reputation to leverage into new markets. In 1949 the product range was expanded to rum and by 1997 Angostura held 97 per cent of the local market share. This consolidated position was used to secure a tie-up with the multinational Bacardi company, and under this arrangement Bacardi purchased all of its rum from Angostura, which was able to gain preferential access to the EU market as a result of Trinidad and Tobago's ACP status. Without its reputation and production leveraged from its consolidated niche, as well as the preferential trading status, this lucrative tie-up might not have materialised.
>
> **Diversification through Acquisition of Strong Brands**
> In 1997 Bacardi sold its stake in Angostura and the company was brought by CL Financial, a Caribbean holding company which gave Angostura the financial backing to expand and diversify further. Importance was attached to a diversification strategy of building production based on strong brands. These brands could not be grown easily from Trinidad and Tobago so a programme of international acquisition was started. In the past five years more companies have been acquired, including Todhunter of the US, which gave access to the US market through its 'Cruzan' brand and Burn Stewart Distillers who produce 'Scottish Leader' whisky, which is popular in Africa. The combined brands use their strength in one market to pull through the other labels in the group. Thus expanding the market presence of each brand is easier.

While it may not be possible for all firms in a small state to reach this level, both these case studies show the potential for enterprises based in small states to become truly globally competitive. Neither had to rely on FDI or on a product based on a unique resource endowment. Instead they simply employed good strategic thought and a mixture of appropriate technology and leverage off the regional market to make the step into global markets. This strategy should be within the reach of all small states' firms.

5.3 Policy and Institutional Factors

The successful recovery of the Trinidadian economy and the move to export competitiveness is the result of a combination of factors – the hard work and success of the individual enterprises, combined with the supporting policy and institutional framework which allowed them to flourish. Some aspects of the policies adopted at that time, and the current institutions, are detailed below.

5.3.1 Policy Framework

The policy framework, developed as a response to the oil price crisis of the 1980s, consisted of a mix of incentive-based policies to remove economic distortions created by past government policies, as well as more active supply side policies to overcome problems that impeded the creation of new competitive advantages by enterprises. While it is not possible to document the entire policy framework here with all its subtle nuances and characteristics, the key features are drawn out below.

Macroeconomic Stability

At the height of the economic crisis caused by the fall in the price of oil, the government appointed a high-level task force to report on the measures needed to produce greater stability and to recommend new policies which were then implemented. These included measures to:

- Tighten monetary policy to retain control of inflation, but balance institutional liquidity;

- Tighten public spending and wage increases, to ensure fiscal sustainability; and

- Devalue and then gradually liberalise the exchange rate to a managed float regime.

Policies have evolved over the years as the situation has improved, but successive governments, from both sides of the political divide, have been committed to implementing and maintaining macroeconomic stability. There is recognition that it is difficult for enterprises to be competitive if the economy within which they are operating is uncertain and uncompetitive, either because of high inflation or rapidly changing interest or exchange rates.

Trade Policy

Like many other developing countries, Trinidad and Tobago pursued a protectionist trade policy based on import substitution, which was achieved through an extensive licensing and quota system. However, while this protected local firms and may have induced some investment, it was a strong disincentive to the encouragement of exports and international competitiveness. As the balance of payments situation worsened at the end of the 1980s the government moved to liberalise the trade regime. Tariff and non-tariff barriers were lowered gradually, to allow firms time to adjust, and following a known and set timetable in order to reduce the power of lobbying. As domestic liberalisation was pursued, so liberalisation of regional markets was sought in order to increase export potential. Trade barriers within CARICOM fell and free trade agreements were sought with South American neighbours.

The changes in trade policy, in conjunction with the other factors detailed in this chapter, have had a significant impact on Trinidad and Tobago's trading profile. The economy is now much more open, with imports and exports as a percentage of GDP increasing from 66 per cent in 1987 to 93 per cent in 2001. The country has also taken advantage of the CARICOM free trade area, almost to a point where it dominates it. In 2001, 66 per cent of total intra-regional exports came from Trinidad and Tobago, while only 6 per cent of intra-regional imports were absorbed by Trinidad and Tobago.[29]

Active Export Promotion Incentives

At the same time as efforts were being made to liberalise the trading regime and achieve macroeconomic stability, policies to actively incentivise exports were also introduced in the short term. These helped to overcome the previous anti-export bias that the previous policy regime had encouraged.

- **Tax Rebates for Retooling:** These provided accelerated depreciation and investment allowances so that 100 per cent of investment on new capital equipment could be depreciated in the year of purchase. Effectively this meant that tax rebates were given for the total amount spent on capital equipment purchase, thereby acting as a huge incentive to retool and boost competitiveness.

- **Tax Allowances for Exports:** Tax free allowances were given as appropriate to the percentage of sales that was exported outside the CARICOM region, i.e. if 50 per cent of sales was exported outside CARICOM, 50 per cent of corporate profits received tax relief.

- **Export Grants for New Market Penetration:** Grants were given to cover 50 per cent of the start-up costs of breaking into new markets outside the CARICOM region. This included the costs of market research/surveillance and of new packaging requirements. The grant only covered expenses until the first commercial shipment was sent.

- **Tax Credits for Ongoing Advertising/Marketing Expenses:** To promote increased promotion in markets outside CARICOM, all advertising and marketing costs were eligible for a 150 per cent tax credit.

It should be noted that due to the introduction of WTO rules to limit export subsidies, direct incentives such as those offered above can no longer be offered solely to exporters. Such incentives must now either be offered equally to all firms or not at all. While only the accelerated depreciation incentive above would still be allowable, the principle of assisting exporters to overcome anti-export bias still holds. This can be achieved to some extent through institutional support (see below).

More Recent Policy Initiatives

Over the years the policy framework has evolved as the economy has recovered, and some policies, such as the active export promotion incentives, have been discontinued. The thrust of the policies however, has been maintained in current policies. Of the more recent policy initiatives, two are of particular interest:

- **Vision 2020:** This is an attempt to set long-term policy goals across a range of policy areas, as well as to pursue realistic implementation plans. Although it is a government-sponsored initiative, the Vision plan involves a wide cross-section of society, including private sector and civil society representatives in all 29 subcommittees and consultation with the public across the country. The process has high level support, with the multisectoral steering group chaired by a leading private sector figure and a Cabinet subcommittee chaired by the Prime Minister. While the process is only at the initial stage, and much work is still to be done designing policy, let alone implementation, it is hoped that this will be the basis for an improved and stable policy environment within which Trinidad and Tobago can become more competitive and raise the standard of living of all its citizens.

- **New Investment Promotion Act:** For a number of years there have been calls from various organisations for the Foreign Investment Act 1990 to be reformed, and the pattern of discretionary investment incentives to be replaced with a simplified lower tax regime that treats foreign and domestic investors equally. A new Act has been drafted, but awaits passage through parliament.

5.3.2 Current SME and Trade Support Institutions

To support the policy framework, a network of SME and trade support institutions have been set up in Trinidad and Tobago with the aim of facilitating growth and encouraging export competitiveness. Over the years the mandate of these institutions has matured and some have been refocused as the economy has evolved; others have been created to fill gaps in the support network. Brief details of three of the institutions involved are given below. Others not covered here, but which are active, include the Free Zones Company, the Export-Import Bank and the Bureau of Standards.

In many ways the current institutional set-up has been designed to match the growth cycle of the enterprises in question. The National Entrepreneurial Development Company (NEDCO) helps with the start-up and incubation of new firms and entrepreneurial spirit, the Business Development Company (BDC) takes established small firms and helps them in the transition to competitive medium size and export-ready status. The Tourism and Development Corporation (TIDCO) then promotes their products overseas, and facilitates information exchange with international markets.

The Tourism and Industrial Development Corporation

TIDCO was set up in 1995 following an amalgamation of three previous institutions for promoting investment, trade and tourism – the Industrial Development Corporation, the Export Development Corporation and the Tourism Development Authority. It now works as a consolidated agency to market and promote Trinidad and Tobago as a premier destination for tourism, investment and a source for quality goods and services – in effect to market and promote 'Brand T&T'. It seeks to focus on promotion and facilitation, rather than micro trade policy issues that should be the realm of the Trade Ministry. In this way it is able to focus its resources more effectively.

TIDCO has approximately 120 employees, of whom 90 are professional staff, an annual operational budget of around $US3.25 million and a capital budget of $US 1.25 million. Given the wide scope of its mandate, it reports to both the Ministry of Tourism and the Ministry of Trade and Industry, and receives its operational budget from the former and its capital expenditure budget from the latter. As TIDCO is the certifying body for various trade agreements, including rules of origin requirements and certification of exporters, it receives income from the required inspections. Currently it receives US$0.4 million annually through such cost recovery.

The Trade and Investment Division of TIDCO has a staff of 28 and a capital budget of almost US$0.5 million. Most of this goes towards trade promotion (US$0.4 million), with the rest (US$0.1 million) being spent on investment promotion. The unit's activities include:

- **Investment Promotion:** Promoting Trinidad and Tobago as an investment location, especially for export competitive industries in the non-oil and non-energy sectors of the economy. This includes facilitating investors through the approval process and then post-investment aftercare.

- **Export Promotion:** Promoting and facilitating the export activities of local manufacturers and producers, including provision of trade information on the criteria, rules and regulations for entering foreign markets. This occurs through traditional promotional outlets (missions, fairs, etc.), as well as increasing use of electronic means such as the web-based trade point system.[30]

- **Research and Analysis:** Conducting sectoral studies, analysis of trade agreements, steps involved in the export process and their cumulative effect on the export sector.

To support and facilitate this work, each year trade and investment promotion missions are arranged to various key markets and exhibition fairs and conferences are organised in Trinidad and Tobago and the region.

The Business Development Company

The BDC started out as the Small Business Development Company (SBDC). At that time it had a broad mandate to support SME development and often acted as a lender of last resort when firms were unable to obtain finance elsewhere. In 2002, however, it was remodelled into a more services focused organisation based on principles of cost recovery, and renamed as the BDC. Its mandate was changed to focus on turning established small businesses into successful medium[31] and large enterprises that can compete more effectively in regional and international markets. To do this the company provides a suite of business development services (technical, financial and export development) to existing businesses on a cost-sharing basis. The aim of these services is to:

- Enhance management capacity;
- Promote technological innovation;
- Encourage product development;
- Improve productivity and quality control; and
- Improve access to export markets for enterprises.

The BDC has a staff of nearly 50 people, approximately 25 of whom are professional staff. It has an operational budget of US$0.8 million, approximately 17 per cent of which comes from cost recovery for services provided. This is targeted to rise to 30 per cent by the end of 2005, through increasing the range of products charged for and the percentage recovery. As an example of present recovery rates, BDC charges 50 per cent of costs for a training session on standards.

The services provided by the BDC include:

- **Training:** Covering a wide range of topics customised as appropriate and including business planning, marketing, standards and ISO awareness raising, and financial management;
- **Consultancy Services:** Advice is given on a wide range of issues, including upgrading, business process re-engineering, sourcing and marketing;
- **Loan Guarantee Scheme:** Guarantees on loans up to US$40,000 if a company's business plan is approved and the applicant contributes some of the capital themselves.

The National Entrepreneurial Development Company

NEDCO was established in 2002, when the SBDC became the BDC, and in effect took over the SBDC's role as an SME start-up incubator. Its mandate is to facilitate and catalyse the development of the SME sector in Trinidad and Tobago by encouraging the development of new small[32] and micro[33] enterprises, particularly among disadvantaged sectors of the community such as young people, women and rehabilitated offenders. This is done through the provision of the following services:

- Entrepreneurial education and development (specialised centres and schools);
- Business advisory and coaching services;
- Business mentoring and training;
- Small loans for business start-ups and advice on securing funding.

Future Challenges for SME and Trade Support Institutions

While the interaction of the network of institutions in Trinidad and Tobago has been designed fairly well from a theoretical point of view, the challenge facing the government and the institutions themselves is to make this work in practice. Care needs to be taken to ensure that activities and initiatives do not overlap, while at the same time ensuring that there are no gaps in the support network. This will require extensive co-ordination between the organisations, at both senior management and operational level, as well as regular monitoring and feedback from users.

A potential problem exists at TIDCO with the desire to combine all promotional efforts into one organisation under 'Brand T&T'. While this does create some synergies, it has perhaps left the organisation trying to do too many things at once, and with confused budgeting and reporting lines. Once the tourism industry has moved out of a phase of needing investment to increase the numbers of hotel rooms available, it may be preferable to split tourism from trade and investment. This would also resolve the problem of reporting to and receiving budgets from two ministries and the inherent conflict of interests that this causes.

5.4 Lessons from Trinidad and Tobago

- **Macro stability is fundamental:** While many factors have been at play in the country's recent success, the role of macroeconomic policy in providing a stable policy environment has been key, especially given the well-documented difficulties that strong oil sector growth can have on the wider economy. With low inflation, a stable exchange rate and sustainable budgets, firms within the economy have had the freedom and incentives to invest and grow.

- **Policy stability and unified strategic direction:** In addition to the stable macro policy environment, the overall strategic direction of policy towards liberalisation, backed by regulatory and supporting institutions, has been maintained by successive governments. This policy stability has helped business planning and given enterprises the confidence to invest. Initiatives such as the Vision 2020 plan can help to reinforce this, as long as they have wide civil society involvement and backing and do not become too politicised.

- **Use the regional market as a stepping stone:** Both the overall trade figures and the individual enterprise case studies point to CARICOM as being an important stepping stone for Trinidad and Tobago in subsequent wider export success. Regional markets offer the opportunity for firms to gain experience in the logistical problems of exporting in a market where the distances involved and the tastes of consumers are perhaps not too different from their own market. This can be invaluable when seeking markets which are further away or more competitive.

- **Encourage retooling and technical innovation:** Within the new manufacturing context discussed in Chapter 2, technology plays a key part. While old and outdated technology may be enough to sustain a niche in the domestic market, if firms are to compete in international markets they need more advanced technology. An example of this can be seen in the case study of S.M. Jaleel, which has used state-of-the-art technology and innovation to create new markets. While ultimately this is a private sector decision, government can encourage retooling and innovation through information sharing and incentive packages, such as accelerated depreciation.

- **Institutional set-up must be clearly defined:** To work effectively, trade support institutions must be integrated into an overall network with an overall strategic purpose. In both the stated mandate and practical operations, areas of overlap need to be eliminated and areas where support is lacking need to be covered. This requires extensive co-ordination between organisations, both at senior management and operational level, as well as regular monitoring and feedback from users.

- **Cost recovery is important, however small the fee:** For the provision of business support and advisory services to work there must be 'buy in' from the enterprises themselves. Making them pay something, however small, is an important concept. However, introducing cost recovery is difficult when recipients are used to free services. To overcome this education is needed on the potential benefits, and the services offered must be desirable and worthwhile.

6

Agenda for Enhancing Competitiveness

A coherent and supportive policy agenda is essential for small states to adjust to globalisation. The new manufacturing context under globalisation exposes enterprises to more intense international competition than ever before, while simultaneously providing access to new markets and global resources (technologies, skills, information and capital). Enterprises face the significant challenge of improving their export capabilities and reaping the benefits of new global markets and resources, while coping with the rigours of open market conditions. The extent of factor market development, as well as past public policies and institutional support, strongly influence the process of capability building at firm level. There are usually both positive and negative aspects to each of these elements and a new policy agenda can help to overcome constraints. This chapter sets out some of the principles which should underlie a competitiveness policy agenda in small states, provides an illustrative agenda and road map for its implementation, and outlines the necessary conditions for success.

6.1 Principles Underlying an Agenda

It is common practice in development economics to draw on available theory and empirical evidence to derive insights for other economies. Building on the analytical framework set out in Chapter 2 and the experiences of Mauritius and Trinidad and Tobago, some broad principles can be put forward to guide the development of an effective long-term competitiveness agenda in small states. Six such principles are suggested:

- Focus on evolving comparative advantage;
- Tailor to national circumstances;
- Link with regional markets and institutions;
- Combine incentives and supply-side measures;
- Involve all major stakeholders; and
- Prioritise interventions and actions.

6.1.1 Focus on Evolving Comparative Advantage
The law of comparative advantage should guide agendas for enhancing competitiveness in small states. For policy purposes it is useful to make a distinction between current and near future comparative advantage. Current comparative advantage suggests specialisa-

tion in the production and export of goods in which a country has a relative cost advantage over others. Near future comparative advantage refers to the export of new goods within a realistic time framework (3–5 years) through the development of new competitive advantages.

The experience of successful small states suggests that radical shifts from one industry to another within a short time span are the exception rather than the rule. Typically, comparative advantage gradually changes over time and supportive competitiveness policies can help this process of evolution. Successful small states have tended initially to concentrate on activities arising from natural resource advantages (for example fish processing, other food products, beverages, tourism related industries, petroleum and related industries) and labour cost advantages (for example textiles and clothing). Once the export momentum is sustained in a core industry (such as textiles and clothing in Mauritius), emphasis shifts to new activities that have a realistic chance of becoming competitive in the near future. Other natural resource based or labour cost based industries may be appropriate at this stage of export development. Over time, industries based on skill and technological advantage may come within the reach of some of the more industrially advanced small states. While it is impossible to predict future patterns of structural change with certainty, it is likely that these patterns will be repeated in other industrial late-comers.

6.1.2 Tailor to National Circumstances

The experiences of more advanced small states and developing countries can offer useful lessons on what works and what does not, and so inform the design of a late-comer's strategy. However, wholesale copying of another country's strategy or relying on a generic one-size-fits-all approach is likely to have a limited effect on improving competitiveness in a given small state. Instead, a competitiveness agenda must be tailored to the circumstances of individual small states and enterprises within them. In particular, it should take into account factors such as geographical location, stage of economic development, macroeconomic and political conditions, the intensity of liberalisation and policy reform, the size and dynamism of the enterprise base, quality of entrepreneurship and industrial skills, and the government's ability to implement policy. Such tailoring is particularly appropriate for micro-states, which may face even more particular circumstances and restricted resources and capabilities than their larger small state neighbours.

6.1.3 Link With Regional Markets and Institutions

Small states' competitiveness agendas should link with regional markets where possible. Regional markets in other developing countries or small states are likely to be less demanding (in their price, quality and delivery requirements) than international markets in developed countries. By focusing on regional markets to begin with, new exporters from small states can accumulate valuable experience of producing for export and then gradually attempt to break into more demanding international markets. Furthermore, such markets may offer other synergies such as foreign direct investment, technology transfer and information. Of course, established exporters, which are already exporting to more demanding international markets, should be encouraged to improve their market penetration and move on to new markets.

Similarly, because they lack their own institutions and resources, small states should take advantage of regional institutions to enhance their competitiveness. Of particular relevance to competitiveness are development banks to provide finance for enterprise development; standards institutions to provide testing, metrology and quality management services; universities to supply tertiary-level technical, managerial and professional skills; and trade negotiation organisations to provide negotiation capabilities to ensure market access. Again, this is particularly true for micro-states, which cannot afford to duplicate all the necessary institutions themselves.

6.1.4 Combine Incentives and Supply-side Measures

The details of the proposed agenda will be set out in Section 6.2. Suffice it to say here that in the past efforts to foster enterprise development were often rather narrowly defined in terms of ensuring macroeconomic stability, open markets and *ad hoc* initiatives to help SMEs, such as establishing an industrial estate or a concessionary credit window. Development experience suggests that this limited approach was insufficient to foster internationally competitive enterprises in small states. It is certainly inadequate to stimulate the start-up and expansion of export-oriented enterprises under today's open and demanding international trading conditions. Thus, a much more complex strategy is required to support export development – involving a mix of incentive policies, supply-side measures and cluster policies – to address the different adjustment needs of enterprises.

6.1.5 Involve All Major Stakeholders

Several stakeholders should be closely involved in formulating an agenda for improving competitiveness. At a minimum, five stakeholder categories should be involved in a competitiveness strategy: enterprises, business associations, trade unions, government and international aid donors. The importance of inclusiveness is largely self-explanatory. The successful preparation of any set of economic policies, including competitiveness strategy, needs a consensus on challenges, goal and broad policy direction among the key social partners affected by those policies.

Each of the five stakeholder groups has valuable inputs – information, experience, finance and mandate – to contribute to competitiveness strategy:

- Enterprises have first-hand experience of the problems affecting business start-up, operation and exporting, and viewpoints on their desired policy and support needs in regard to export incentives, finance and non-financial support services.

- Business associations can offer additional insights on these issues in relation to particular industrial and service sectors, as well as articulate the special needs of vulnerable groups of enterprises (for example gender, ethnic minorities or young people).

- Trade unions represent the interest of labour and help with awareness raising and skills upgrading during enterprise restructuring.

- It is usually the responsibility of government to design and implement a strategy for improving competitiveness in consultation with other actors.

- Donor agencies can support these initiatives by providing technical assistance, best practice experience and foreign aid.

6.1.6 Prioritise Interventions and Actions

Given the limited resources available to many small states, it is vital that the implementation of any competitiveness strategy is properly prioritised to ensure maximum returns and to prevent reform fatigue setting in before crucial changes are made. This should be done in line with the particular circumstances of the country involved, taking into account both political and economic characteristics and the realities on the ground. Guidance for such prioritisation should come from the type of diagnostic study set out in Section 6.3 below.

6.2 An Illustrative Agenda

Using the six principles set out in Section 6.1, an illustrative long-term competitiveness agenda can be formulated for a typical small state.[34] This task may appear difficult at first because of a myriad of possible policy instruments and support measures that are available at national, sector and firm level to address the competitiveness challenge.

6.2.1 Types of Policy Instrument and Support Measures

To aid analysis, the various policy instruments and support measures can be grouped under three distinct headings:[35]

Incentive policies that seek to remove economic distortions created by past government policies which discouraged enterprise growth and competitiveness. Incentive policies are often equated with liberalisation and stabilisation measures proposed by international financial institutions and associated with economic reform programmes. Measures for controlling inflation and ensuring macroeconomic stability, elimination of quantitative restrictions, tariff reform, tax incentives, a competitive real exchange rate, export incentives and promotion, streamlining of bureaucratic procedures on enterprise activity and exporting and privatisation of public enterprises all fall under this heading.

Supply-side policies geared to overcome systems failures, which impede collective learning processes and the creation of new competitive advantages by enterprises. These include a variety of support for enterprises including investments in human resources, fostering small and medium enterprises, technological support, attracting foreign investment and facilitating technology transfer from abroad, promotion of e-commerce, ensuring access to industrial finance, strengthening private sector associations and improving infrastructure. This heading involves largely non-sector specific measures.

Cluster policies, which emphasise detailed actions to improve the competitiveness of specific industrial clusters (involving SMEs and other firms) in a small state. Intervention is directed towards acquiring technological capabilities, promoting upgrading and improving links between different parts of the cluster. Policies might range from industry-specific tax measures to the provision of specialised institutional support facilities for a particular cluster. Joint actions (for example setting up a specialised training school) between a business association in the cluster and an aid donor or a government agency are also commonplace.

The design and implementation of effective cluster policies requires sophisticated government capabilities to collect information, design appropriate micro-level interventions, work closely with the private sector to implement such policies, and monitor and evaluate the results. Small states, which often lack these government capabilities due to their small size, face a high risk of government failure in the sense of poorly designed and implemented cluster policies. Given this risk of wasting limited resources, until such time as government capabilities have been built up to appropriate levels, cluster policies should be used sparingly in small states and the focus of intervention should be on incentive and supply-side measures.

6.2.2 Example Agenda

Table 6.1 contains a policy agenda for small states which sets out key objectives and illustrative examples of incentive policies and supply-side measures. Many of these measures have been adapted to the economic needs of small states. For instance, emphasis is given to promotion of e-commerce and the development of infrastructure to remedy the geographical isolation of some small states from overseas markets. The development of linkages with regional institutions (for example trade negotiations, education and standards) is highlighted to maximise regional synergies and externalities. Significant attention is given to the promotion of small and medium enterprises, which form the industrial backbone of many small states. Human development is fundamental, as an educated and creative labour force is the main resource of small states and their enterprises. Attracting foreign investment and providing adequate technological support are essential in a world of rapidly changing technologies. Strong private sector associations and regular public–private sector dialogues assist the formulation of policies geared to private sector needs and long-run policy coherence.

All the suggestions for the policy agenda set out in Table 6.1 are consistent with a broad outward-oriented, market-friendly development strategy. It is worth underlining that it is the *interaction* of incentive and supply-side measures (as well as cluster policies) that determine competitiveness in small states, rather than a single category of measures. It should also be noted that the policy agenda is only illustrative and will not be appropriate for the specific situation of every small state. Section 6.3 details how the agenda can be developed to fit the circumstances and needs of a given small state.

6.3 An Implementation Road Map

Clearly all the measures contained in the illustrative agenda in Table 6.1 are not applicable to the specific situation of every small state. For instance, some small states may have already implemented some of these measures, some measures may not be relevant to some small states and new measures may be required which are not shown in the table. Hence, there is a need to develop an agenda that fits the circumstances and needs of a given small state. This requirement will be particularly pertinent for micro-states, which may have even more specific needs and constraints.

This process of tailoring competitiveness strategy to the individual small state can be guided by a simple road map. The road map set out in Figure 6.1 is made up of four phases, each building on previous efforts: inception review, assessing competitiveness, designing strategy and sustaining competitiveness. These steps and the issue of a co-ordinating department are discussed further below:

Inception: In order to fully understand the specific challenges and problems likely to be encountered in the exercise, it is necessary to undertake several inception tasks. These include a preliminary stocktaking of past reports and policy initiatives; undertaking consultations with relevant stakeholders (for example key government departments, private sector organisations, trade unions and aid donors); allocating finance and setting a budget for the project; developing detailed terms of reference for activities; assigning responsibilities; engaging consultants as required; assigning government counterparts; and developing a timetable for implementation. The output of this phase will be a short inception study. A workshop of key stakeholders should be held to discuss the report and chart the way forward.

Assessing competitiveness: The basis for designing an overarching competitiveness agenda for improving performance in a given small state is a comprehensive assessment of competitiveness patterns and policies. The assessment would make use of existing studies, as well as commissioned enterprise surveys, institutional reviews and policy analysis.

Table 6.1: A Policy Matrix for Small States

Objectives	Policy Options
1. Maintain credible macroeconomic policies and exchange rate flexibility.	• Fine-tune fiscal and monetary policy to provide reasonably predictable low inflation and steady growth in the macroeconomic environment. • Rationalise public expenditure by limiting the growth of the wage bill, reducing government employment and privatising poorly performing state enterprises. • Extend the tax base, rationalise taxes and reduce economically inefficient subsidies. • Adopt a proactive approach to exchange rate management to ensure a competitive real exchange rate.
2. Persist with outward-oriented trade policies.	• Eliminate quantitative restrictions and reduce import tariffs in a pre-announced, phased manner to achieve low uniform effective protection across activities. • Improve access to imported inputs by making customs procedures more efficient. • Establish a well-resourced trade and investment promotion agency (with private sector board) with a mandate to develop and implement an export promotion strategy. • Provide part grants for export-ready SMEs to develop websites and to participate in overseas trade fairs and buyer-seller meets. • Establish a network of shops for tourists as joint ventures between SME associations and the trade and investment promotion organisation. • Integrate national trade negotiations capacity with regional negotiating machinery to maximise available resources, economic and legal skills and information.
3. Foster small business start-up and growth.	• Set a low corporation tax rate and, where feasible and economically viable, extend tax coverage to all businesses, including SMEs. • Streamline procedures affecting business start-up (for example registration) and operation to reduce transactions costs on business • Improve access to credit by improving collateral procedures (for example a debt tribunal separate from the court system), starting-up credit registries to improve lending quality and quantity and a micro-finance scheme. • Explore the establishment of a regional credit guarantee scheme to facilitate commercial bank lending to small businesses. • Lobby for significant increase in regional development bank concessionary lending for small business. • Establish an SME agency (with a private sector board) to provide business advisory services, entrepreneur training, information services and common facilities. • Develop a common definition of SMEs (for example the number of employees) and collect and monitor information on SME performance.

Table 6.1 (continued)

	Objectives	Policy Options
4.	Invest in human resources	• Improve quality of secondary schools by allocating funds based on enrolments; give special grants to schools with large needs (for example a large proportion of students reading below grade); create incentives for attracting qualified teachers to teach in schools with below average school results; make school results public; and give more emphasis to maths, science, IT and business education in the school curriculum. • Upgrade vocational training facilities and gear up courses to industrial needs. • Encourage training in SMEs through a public information campaign to make them aware of skill gaps for competitiveness and provide subsidised consultancy services for in-plant training. • Start a programme to improve work ethics and reduce absenteeism in skilled and unskilled labour. • Introduce incentives to attract back professionally qualified nationals from overseas. • Streamline the work permit system to enable easier entry of professional and technical manpower and certain categories of skilled workers.
5.	Ensure adequate technological support	• Set up a scheme to part finance the cost of consultancy services for ISO 9000 and 14000 certification for SMEs. • Upgrade the capacity of the national standards bureau to provide testing, metrology, quality management, productivity and other technical services to international standards. Formally link national standards bureau to regional standards organisation (or an international standards organisation) to facilitate continuous technology and skill transfer. Aggressively market technical services to SMEs. • Provide information services to permit ready access to specialist regional and international technical consultants as required. • Promote awareness among SMEs of the need to upgrade their technological capabilities and invest in new equipment.
6.	Encourage and increase inflows of foreign direct investment	• Provide the trade and investment promotion agency with a mandate to develop and implement a targeted investment promotion strategy. • Develop a new investment incentive package based on low corporation tax rates for established activities and limited tax holidays for new activities (for example 5–10 years). • Streamline foreign investment approvals by creating a single-stage approval process and setting a rapid target for normal approvals (for example two weeks). • Liberalise and overhaul work permit regulations for entrepreneurs, technical and professional manpower, and selected categories of skilled workers. • Lobby international financial institutions to create an international investment guarantee scheme to reduce risks of inward investment in small states.

Table 6.1 (continued)

Objectives	Policy Options
7. Improve private sector associations.	• Encourage SMEs to establish associations in leading export sectors. • Promote the establishment of a federation of SME export associations to hold a dialogue with government on economic policy issues and provide some support services to members, for example training and market information.
8. Strengthen public–private sector dialogue and partnerships.	• Initiate annual consultations between government ministers and business leaders on economic policy questions, for example pre-budget consultations. • Involve private sector representatives in trade negotiations and investment promotion. • Set up a secondment programme for experienced private sector managers to work in government departments for up to one year.
9. Promote e-commerce and e-government.	• Liberalise local telecommunications industry to reduce costs and increase efficiency. • Expand bandwidth on local and international backbone; develop interoperability standards; and administer a top-level domain country code. • Develop a programme to encourage universal adoption of internet-linked computers in homes and businesses. • Overhaul relevant legislation to permit e-commerce. • Formulate an e-government strategy with clear objectives and phased measures. • Facilitate on-line payments for all government services. • Upgrade IT systems in government departments and conduct training for civil services.
10. Improve quality and coverage of infrastructure.	• Explore the feasibility of increasing air flights and cargo capacity from regional and international carriers. • Improve roads and water services by levying and increasing tolls and user fees. • Upgrade port facilities including container handling and refrigeration facilities to the best regional standards.

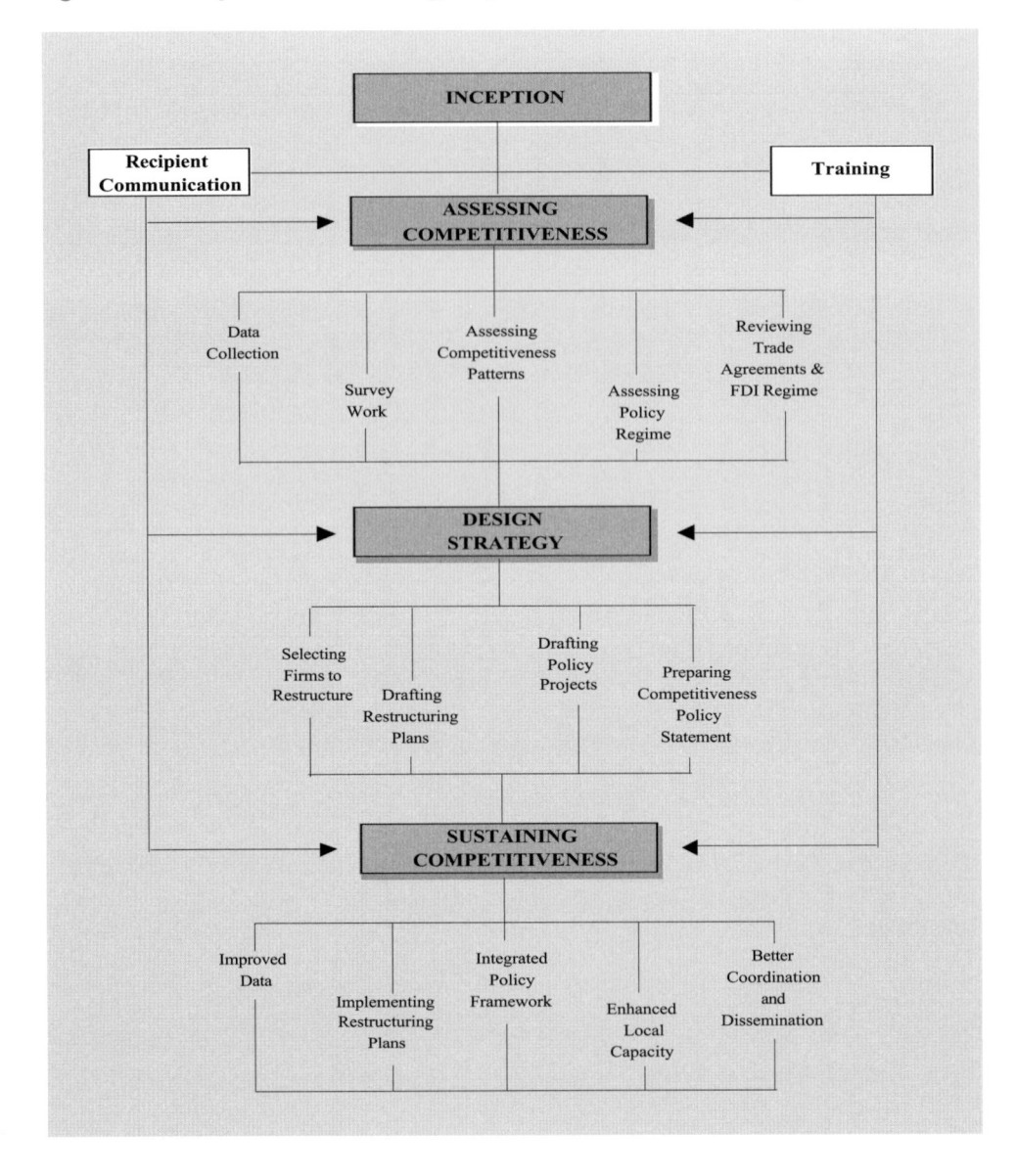

Figure 6.1: Competitiveness Strategy Implementation – A Road Map

```
                            INCEPTION
  ┌──────────────┐              │                        ┌──────────┐
  │  Recipient   │──────────────┼────────────────────────│ Training │
  │Communication │         ASSESSING                     └──────────┘
  └──────────────┘──────▶ COMPETITIVENESS ◀──────────────
                              │
         ┌────────────────────┼────────────────────┐
       Data            Assessing                Reviewing
     Collection       Competitiveness             Trade
                        Patterns               Agreements &
              Survey              Assessing      FDI Regime
               Work                Policy
                                   Regime

                            DESIGN
                    ───▶   STRATEGY   ◀───
                              │
         ┌────────────────────┼────────────────────┐
      Selecting          Drafting
      Firms to            Policy             Preparing
     Restructure         Projects          Competitiveness
              Drafting                         Policy
            Restructuring                     Statement
              Plans

                          SUSTAINING
                    ───▶ COMPETITIVENESS ◀───
                              │
         ┌────────────────────┼────────────────────┐
      Improved           Integrated             Better
        Data               Policy            Coordination
                         Framework               and
            Implementing           Enhanced  Dissemination
            Restructuring           Local
              Plans                Capacity
```

A variety of quantitative and qualitative techniques should be employed to analyse the information. The assessment would attempt to do the following:

- Identify trends in industrial competitiveness at sector and product level;
- Map out in key sectors firm-level technological, marketing and other export capabilities relative to international and developing country best practice;

- The stability of the macroeconomic environment,, including growth, inflation and the real exchange rate;
- Assess policy and regulatory impacts including simulation analysis;
- Evaluate trade agreements and patterns of foreign investment;
- The availability and quality of human resources, particularly skill gaps, and labour market conditions, including wages and productivity;
- Sources, terms and access to industrial finance;
- The adequacy of services and support provided by technology institutions;
- The quality and cost competitiveness of physical infrastructure;
- The capacity of the lead ministry to undertake policy co-ordination.

The output of this phase will be a detailed competitiveness study which should contain broad policy suggestions. Another workshop of key stakeholders should be conducted to analyse the current situation, debate policy options and formulate an agreed agenda.

Designing strategy: Drawing on the analytical phases of the work described above and with further consultations with relevant stakeholders, a series of tailored policy projects will be developed. These policy projects should address generic and specific competitiveness issues that affect enterprises and the business environment. Examples are given in Table 6.1. A useful way of consolidating these projects would be to present them in the form of an overarching document – a competitiveness policy statement. Apart from presenting detailed policy suggestions, the statement should also contain headline budgets for activities, a timetable for implementation, milestones and indicators to assess progress, and responsibilities for implementing activities to given institutions (and officers within them). More complex and detailed competitiveness strategies sometimes also provide for restructuring plans for selected enterprises, particularly for public enterprises. Where this is the case, headline information on these plans could be included in the competitiveness policy statement. Widespread consultations with stakeholders will assist in building a national consensus on the objectives of the statement and the policy projects.

Sustaining competitiveness: Next comes the challenge of taking forward the agreed policy statement, requiring determination, hard work and political will. A wide range of activities will be involved in this phase, including:

- Implementing restructuring plans and policy projects;
- Integrating policy initiatives so that they are complementary;

- Proposing and drafting legislation to enact policy changes;
- Training and capacity building in both the government and private sector;
- Co-ordination and dissemination of findings; and
- Continuous monitoring and evaluation of progress and adapting initiatives as required.

Co-ordinating department: Designing and implementing a competitiveness strategy requires closely integrated actions by a number of government departments and agencies. It is essential that a single department is entrusted with co-ordinating the process of competitiveness strategy development and implementation. Without some co-ordination there is a risk that the process may lose momentum. Possible candidates for this co-ordinating role include:

- The Ministry of Trade and Industry;
- The Ministry of Finance;
- The Prime Minister's office.

With its mandate to formulate trade and industrial policies, specialised expertise and close links with the business community, the Ministry of Trade and Industry would be the obvious choice. However, it may require enhanced functions, more resources and capacity building to undertake this role. Where a separate Ministry of Trade and Industry does not exist (or is deemed to be too weak to be effective), the Ministry of Finance may be more appropriate. In some rare circumstances, the Prime Minister's office may be the best candidate.

6.4 Conditions for Success

A coherent competitiveness strategy, along with a good implementation plan, is a necessary but not sufficient condition for long-run export success in small states. The economic development record of small states suggests that other factors are required to support even the best-designed competitiveness strategies. Some of these factors are illustrated in Figure 6.2.

They fall into two categories.

- The first are external factors that originate outside an economy. External factors can have a significant impact on the outcome of a competitiveness strategy in a small state, but are often outside the direct scope of national policy-making. They could include shocks such as financial crises, natural disasters and terrorism. They could also include international rules and obligations under organisations such as the WTO or the IMF. While such agreements and rules can be positive or negative depending on the circumstances, they reduce the available policy space and restrict government's ability to determine policy and influence the outcome of a competitiveness strategy.

- The second are factors that are internal to a small economy and within the scope of the influence of national policy-making. Many of these issues fall within the heading of governance, which is a separate topic that requires further analysis for small states. Whilst a full examination of governance is beyond the scope of this study, some of the issues are discussed briefly below.

Figure 6.2: Conditions for Success

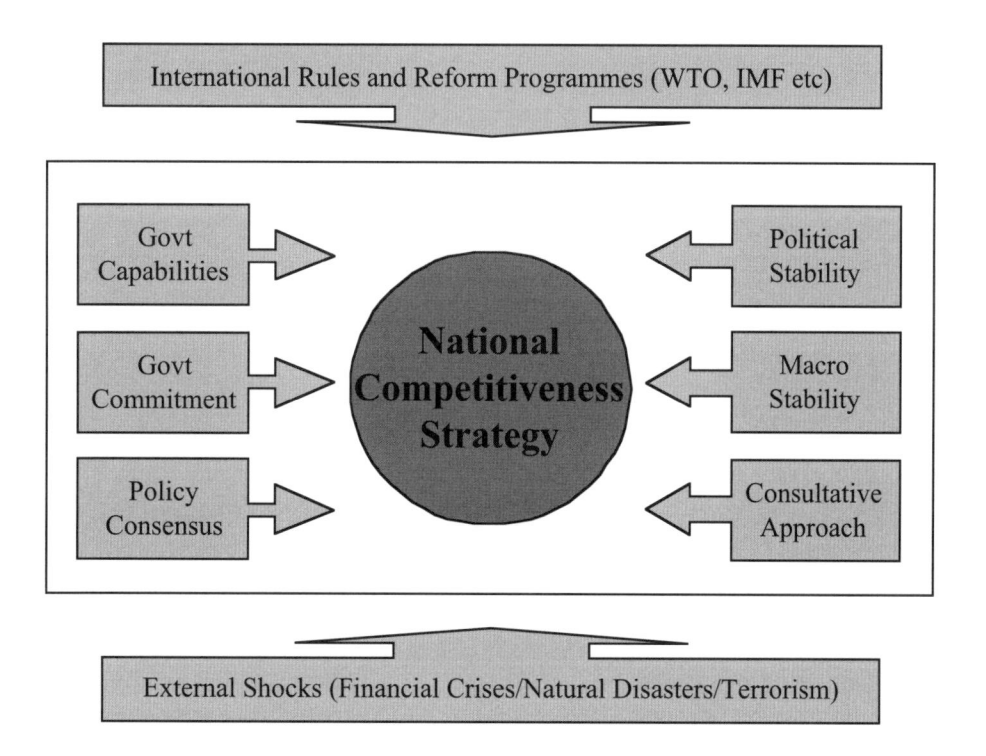

```
        ┌──────────────────────────────────────────────────────┐
        │  International Rules and Reform Programmes (WTO, IMF etc)│
        └──────────────────────────────────────────────────────┘

  ┌─────────────┐                                    ┌─────────────┐
  │    Govt     │ ⇨                                ⇦ │  Political  │
  │ Capabilities│                                    │  Stability  │
  └─────────────┘         ⬤ National                 └─────────────┘
  ┌─────────────┐        Competitiveness             ┌─────────────┐
  │    Govt     │ ⇨       Strategy                 ⇦ │    Macro    │
  │ Commitment  │                                    │  Stability  │
  └─────────────┘                                    └─────────────┘
  ┌─────────────┐                                    ┌─────────────┐
  │   Policy    │ ⇨                                ⇦ │ Consultative│
  │  Consensus  │                                    │  Approach   │
  └─────────────┘                                    └─────────────┘

        ┌──────────────────────────────────────────────────────┐
        │ External Shocks (Financial Crises/Natural Disasters/Terrorism)│
        └──────────────────────────────────────────────────────┘
```

Political stability: Civil conflict, domestic political violence and international disputes significantly reduce a government's capacity to undertake competitiveness strategies. Defence expenditure is often increased at the expense of foreign investment, export promotion and technology support budgets. Key policy-makers are sometimes switched from economic management to crisis management. Negotiations with arms dealers and aid donors can assume a higher priority than a dialogue with the private sector over competitiveness strategy or a focus on policy implementation and monitoring. Moreover, the country's reputation suffers as a destination for foreign investment and foreign buyers may seek out more reliable suppliers. Country reputations and international goodwill are 'a scarce national resource' and can take many decades and many millions of dollars in promotion campaigns to rebuild.

Sound macroeconomic performance: Good macroeconomic conditions assist the implementation of national competitiveness strategies while macroeconomic crises are a hindrance. Difficulties in containing inflation, sudden exchange rate devaluation or domestic recession often contribute to reversals in certain aspects of competitiveness policies after their implementation, including the reimposition of exchange controls or import controls and cuts in expenditure on education and training.

Strong government capabilities: While there is a theoretical case for public action to enhance competitiveness, in practice governments may lack the requisite skills and information to formulate, implement and monitor such strategies. Undertaking detailed national competitiveness strategies (involving carefully designed foreign investment targeting, export contests, training programmes and technology development schemes) demands a host of economic, management engineering and information technology skills that are in short supply in many developing country civil services. In part this may be due to civil service recruitment practices and compensation schemes which typically focus on recruiting generalists and giving them on-the-job training rather than hiring specialists with relevant private sector experience.

Sustained government commitment: Owing in part to their concern with structural issues (for example skills, technology and institutional reforms) competitiveness policies can take time to show results. Inadequate commitment by government has often limited the seriousness of policy implementation and backsliding has sometimes affected sustainability. Changing governments and leaders, and internal opposition to changes within government, have frequently led to policy reversals.

Consultative approach and policy consensus: Successful implementation of a competitiveness strategy will require the government to adopt a consultative approach and maintain good relations with the private sector, trade unions and wider civil society. The political and economic history of a country can hinder the success of such an approach and may have to be worked at to ensure that an inclusive approach is adopted and that policy consensus is reached. For example, a government with a 'socialist overhang' is likely to regard the private sector with suspicion, particularly multinational affiliates, and may not seek their advice on economic policy matters and implementation issues. Similarly, countries that have had a long period of inward-looking policies may be characterised by a tiny private sector with limited industrial experience. Such an 'infant private sector' is unlikely to have the requisite technological and marketing capabilities to respond quickly to changes in incentive policies or to have the relevant international exposure to advise government on good competitiveness policies.

6.5 A Last Word

Small states face significant challenges in an ever more open and globalised world, especially given that they are potentially more vulnerable than other states. However, as has been shown throughout this report, there are success stories among the small states, and rather than concentrating purely on vulnerability many would benefit from a more proactive approach to improving competitiveness through concerted policy action. There are no magic wands in economic development, and achieving success will take years of hard work, but small states that tackle the constraints identified, and design and implement a coherent competitiveness strategy will have the best chance of long-term success.

Notes

1. Detailed competitiveness studies on individual small states include: World Bank (1994) on Mauritius; Harris (1997) on Jamaica; Lall and Wignaraja (1998) on Mauritius; and Malta Ministry of Economic Services (1999) on Malta.
2. An exception is Easterly and Kraay (2001). Using cross-country regression analysis, they test whether small states are any different from large states in terms of their income, growth and volatility outcomes. They find that small states have significantly higher per capita incomes than others and that there is no significant difference in the growth performance between large and small states. Although conceding that small states suffer from greater growth volatility and terms of trade shocks due to openness, they argue that the net benefits of openness are positive. They conclude that small states are no different from large states and so should not receive different policy advice.
3. See, for instance, CBD/CAIC (2002) for a range of popular views on competitiveness in the Caribbean.
4. For academic variants of these popular views see Harris (1997) and Wint (2003).
5. For recent surveys of this literature see Kim and Nelson (2000) and Wignaraja (2003).
6. Lall (1992); Bell and Pavitt (1993); Wignaraja (1998); Radosevic (1999); Mytelka (1999); Levy, Berry and Nugent (1999).
7. A firm's technology strategy will vary according to its own stage of technological development. Mytelka (1999) distinguishes between three strategies: catch-up strategy, keep-up strategy and get-ahead strategy, which correspond to the late-comer stage, quick-follower stage and front-runner stage of a technological learning approach. She argues that the three different strategies, each with different objectives, require different types of knowledge for upgrading and different sources of such knowledge. This suggests that is important for a learning SME to be able to assess its own technological capability objectively and adopt a phased approach to technological development.
8. For more on NIS see the classic work by Lundvall (1992). See also Metcalfe (2003).
9. The UNCTAD/WTO International Trade Centre also produces a Trade Performance Index, which benchmarks across developing countries at an industry/product level (ITC, 2000). Whilst it is not discussed here due to our focus on national-level competitiveness, for policy-makers interested in such detail it can be a useful tool.
10. Technology intensive exports include electronics, petrochemicals and chemicals, iron and steel, engineering and plastics.
11. Swaziland's large share of manufacturing in GDP seems due to the following: (a) 26 garment factories established by Taiwanese investors to take advantage of the African Growth and Opportunities Act which provides ready access to the American market; (b) the presence of one of Coca Cola's five plants worldwide which produces cola concentrate; (c) various sugar pulp factories; and (d) other light industries established by South African investors to take advantage of the South African Customs Union market.
12. Calculations were also done including Singapore, Taiwan and Costa Rica, in order to check the robustness of the theory, and to give a context to the SSMECI figures. Not surprisingly, these countries came out at the top of the index.
13. Of the 47 small states in our definition, seven countries could not be included in the final MECI for data reasons; five of these were in the Pacific. As a result, the sample for the Pacific is not complete and may be biased. However, lack of data is often correlated to poor performance, and it is unlikely that inclusion of these countries, if data was available, would significantly improve overall regional performance.
14. Attempts at statistical analysis of the factors affecting competitiveness in developing countries include Ul Haque (1995); James and Romijn (1997); Wignaraja (1999); Wignaraja and Taylor (2003); and Wint (2003).
15. An important qualification about the testing procedure should be noted. The simple t-test shows significantly different means between two samples for individual variables. However, it does not indicate causality, and is thus less powerful than full econometric analysis. That said, it does provide insights into those underlying factors correlated with competitive success in comparisons of strong and weak national performance.
16. 'Classification of Economies by Size', in B. Jalan (1987).
17. With regression analysis, one can analyse how a single dependent variable is affected by the values of one or more independent variables – for example, how a small state's performance is affected by such factors as country size, export orientation and FDI inflows. Shares in the performance measure can be apportioned to each of these three factors, based on a set of performance data. Simple linear regression was used in Table 3.10 rather than multiple regression due to the likelihood of pervasive multicolinearity problems between the independent variables.
18. The Human Development Index is produced annually by the UNDP. It uses a weighted sum of three indices

representing life expectancy, educational attainment and adjusted GDP per capita. For each country, each of the three variables is indexed to a value between 0 and 1, and then the three indices are combined with equal weights to form the HDI.

19 For recent accounts see World Bank (1994); Lall and Wignaraja (1998); ILO (1999); UNCTAD (2000); Subramanian and Roy (2001); Treebhoohun (2001); and Wignaraja (2002).
20 See UNIDO (2003) and Wignaraja and Taylor (2003) for examinations of Africa's industrial competitiveness record in a comparative perspective. The best performances include Tunisia, Morocco, South Africa and Mauritius.
21 See Subramanian and Roy (2001) p. 6.
22 For an account of the growth of the sugar and tourism sectors in Mauritius see Woldekidan (1994) and Government of Mauritius (1997).
23 See Woldekidan (1994); World Bank (1994); Lall and Wignaraja (1998); Teal (1999); and Durbarry (2001).
24 Data on inflation (Consumer Price Index) confirms Mauritius' record in macroeconomic management. Inflation rates averaged 7.7 per cent per year in the period 1980–2001. The period average masks more recent success. Inflation rates fell from 13 per cent per year in 1974–1984 to 7.4 per cent in 1985–1994 and further to 6.2 per cent per year in 1995–2002. Source: World Bank, *World Development Indicators*.
25 Apart from the organisations listed here, there is also the Mauritius Standards Bureau which provides metrology, standards and quality services; the National Computer Board which provides support to the IT industry; the University of Mauritius which conducts tertiary-level education; and the National Productivity and Competitiveness Council which is engaged in awareness raising about productivity issues.
26 A recent study found that annual wages in Mauritius manufacturing went up threefold from US$1063 to US$2998 between 1985 and 1993. The country's 1993 wages were four times higher than Sri Lanka's and China's, three times higher than Bangladesh's and twice those of India and Indonesia. The enterprise survey in the same study reported that 61 per cent of firms felt that the decline in labour productivity was a negative constraint on competitiveness. See Lall and Wignaraja (1998).
27 The negative effects of over-reliance on natural resources has been named 'Dutch Disease' following The Netherlands' experience with North Sea gas. For a fuller explanation of this see Corden (1984).
28 In constant 1995 US$.
29 Caricom Secretariat Online Statistics Database – Selected Economic Statistics.
30 See *www.tradetnt.com* for more details.
31 In Trinidad and Tobago, medium-sized enterprises are defined as those employing 26–50 people, with assets of TT$1.5–5 million (US$0.25–0.8 million) and with sales of TT$5–10 million (US$0.8–1.6 million).
32 A small enterprise is defined as a company which employs 6–25 persons, with assets valued between TT$250,000–1.5 million (US$40,000–250,000) and sales worth TT$250,000–5 million (US$40,000–0.8 million).
33 Micro-enterprises are defined as employing one to five persons, with less than TT$250,000 (US$40,000) in assets and less than TT$250,000 (US$40,000) in sales.
34 Recent examples include Trinidad and Tobago Ministry of Enterprise Development and Foreign Affairs (2001); Malta Ministry of Economic Services (1999); Lall and Wignaraja (1998) for Mauritius; World Bank (2003) for Jamaica.
35 For more discussion of these concepts, see Wignaraja (2003a).

Bibliography

ADB (1998). *Improving Growth Prospects in the Pacific*, Manila: Asian Development Bank.

ADB (2003). 'Special Chapter: Competitiveness in Developing Asia' in *Asian Development Outlook 2003*, Oxford: Oxford University Press.

Atkins, J.P., Mazzi, S. and Easter, C.D. (2001). 'Small States: A Composite Vulnerability Index' in Peretz, D., Faruqi, R. and Kissanga, E. (eds), *Small States in the Global Economy*, London: Commonwealth Secretariat, pp. 53–92.

Bell, M. and Pavitt, K. (1993). 'Technological Accumulation and Industrial Growth: Contrasts Between Developed and Developing Countries', *Industrial and Corporate Change* 2 (2): 157–210.

Bernal, R.L. (2001). 'Globalisation and Small Developing Economies: Challenges and Opportunities' in Peretz, D., Faruqi, R. and Kissanga, E. (eds), *Small States in the Global Economy*, London: Commonwealth Secretariat, pp. 53–91.

Briguglio, L. (1995). 'Small Island Developing States and their Economic Vulnerabilities', *World Development* 23 (9): 1615–32.

CBD/CAIC (2002). 'Private Sector Summit 2002: Competitive Private Sector Development – An Imperative for the Future', Report on Proceedings of a Joint Caribbean Development Bank (CBD)/Caribbean Association of Industry and Commerce (CAIC) Workshop, 4 March 2002, Grand Barbados Beach Resort, Barbados.

Collier, P. and Dollar, D. (2001). 'Aid, Risk and the Special Concerns of Small States' in Peretz, D., Faruqi, R. and Kissanga, E. (ed.), *Small States in the Global Economy*, London: Commonwealth Secretariat, pp. 11–38.

Corden W.M. (1984). 'Booming Sector and Dutch Disease Economics: Survey and Consolidation', *Oxford Economic Papers*, Vol. 36, pp. 359–80.

Commonwealth Consultative Group (1985). *Vulnerability: Small States in the Global Society*, London: Commonwealth Secretariat.

Commonwealth Secretariat (1997). *A Future for Small States: Overcoming Vulnerability*, Report of a Commonwealth Advisory Group, London: Commonwealth Secretariat.

Crafts, N. (2000). 'Globalisation and Growth in the Twentieth Century', IMF Working Paper No. 00/44.

Dabee, R. (2002). 'The Role of Non-Traditional Exports in Mauritius', in Helleiner, G.K. (ed.), *Non-Traditional Exports in Sub-Saharan Africa: Issues and Experiences*, Basingstoke, UK: Palgrave, pp. 135–61.

Dabee, R. and Greenaway, D. (eds) (2001). *The Mauritian Economy: A Reader*, Basingstoke, UK: Palgrave.

De Chazal Du Mee (1998). 'Research Study on Small and Medium Enterprises in Mauritius: First Interim Report', Port Louis: De Chazal Du Mee.

Dubarry, R. (2001). 'The Export Processing Zone' in Dabee, R. and Greenaway, D. (eds), *The Mauritian Economy: A Reader*, Basingstoke, UK: Palgrave.

Easterly, W. and Kraay, A. (2001). 'Small States, Small Problems? Income, Growth and Volatility in Small States' in Peretz, D., Faruqi, R. and Kissanga, E. (eds), *Small States in the Global Economy*, London: Commonwealth Secretariat, pp. 93–116.

Fagerberg, J. (1996). 'Technology and Competitiveness', *Oxford Review of Economic Policy* 12(3): 39–51.

Ghose, A.K. (2003). *Jobs and Incomes in a Globalising World*, Geneva: International Labour Office.

Grynberg, R. (2001). 'Trade Policy Implications for Small Vulnerable States of the Global Trade Regime Shift' in Peretz, D., Faruqi, R. and Kissanga, E. (eds), *Small States in the Global Economy*, London: Commonwealth Secretariat, pp. 267–328.

Harris, D.J. (1997). *Jamaica's Export Economy: Towards a Strategy of Export-Led Growth*, (Critical Issues in Caribbean Development Series, No. 5) Kingston: Ian Randle Publishers.

Holden, P., Bale, M. and Holden, S. (2004). *Swimming against the Tide: An Assessment of the Private Sector in the Pacific*, Pacific Studies Series, Manila: Asian Development Bank.

Howard, M. (2002). 'Causality between exports, imports and income in Trinidad and Tobago', *International Economic Journal* 16:4, 97–106, University of the West Indies.

Hughes, A. and Brewster, H. (2002). *Lowering the Threshold*, Commonwealth Economic Paper No. 50, London: Commonwealth Secretariat.

ILO (1999). *Studies in the Social Dimension of Globalisation: Mauritius*, Geneva: International Labour Organisation.

IMD (2003). *The World Competitiveness Yearbook 2003*, Lausanne: International Institute for Management Development.

ITC (2000a). *Redefining Trade Promotion: The Need for a Strategic Response*, Geneva: UNCTAD/WTO International Trade Centre.

ITC (2000b). 'The Trade Performance Index: Background Paper', Geneva: UNCTAD/WTO International Trade Centre, Market Analysis Section.

James, J. and Romijn, H. (1997). 'The Determinants of Technological Capability: A Cross-Country Analysis', *Oxford Development Studies*, Vol. 25, No. 2, pp. 189–207.

Jalan, B. (ed.) 1987). *Problems and Policies in Small Economies*, London: Croom Helm.

Jessen, A. and Rodriguez, E. (1999). 'The Caribbean Community: Facing the Challenges of Regional and Global Integration', *INTAL-ITD Occasional Paper 2* (Institute for the Integration of Latin America and the Caribbean, INTAL and Inter-American Development Bank, IDB). www.iadb.org/int/pub

Kim, L. and Nelson R.R. (eds) (2000). *Technological Learning and Economic Development: The Experience of the Asian NIEs*, Cambridge: Cambridge University Press.

Krugman, P. (1996). 'Making Sense of the Competitiveness Debate', *Oxford Review of Economic Policy* 12(3): 17–25.

Lall, S. (2001a). *Competitiveness, Technology and Skills*, Aldershot, UK: Edward Elgar.

Lall, S. (1992). 'Technological Capabilities and Industrialisation', *World Development* 20: 65–186.

Lall, S. (2001b). 'Competitiveness Indices and Developing Countries: An Economic Evaluation of the Global Competitiveness Report', *World Development* 29(9): 1501–25.

Lall, S. and Wignaraja, G. (1994). 'Foreign Involvement by European Firms and Garment Exports By Developing Countries', *Asia-Pacific Development Journal* 1(2).

Lall, S. and Wignaraja, G. (1998). *Mauritius: Dynamising Export Competitiveness*, Commonwealth Economic Paper No. 33, Commonwealth Secretariat: London.

Lamusse, R. (1995), 'Mauritius', in Wangwe, S. (ed.), *Exporting Africa: Technology, Trade and Industrialisation in Sub-Saharan Africa*, London: Routledge, pp. 350–75.

Levy, B., Berry, A. and Nugent, J.B. (1999). *Fulfilling the Export Potential of Small and Medium Firms*, Boston: Kluwer Academic Publishers.

Lundvall, B-A. (ed.) (1992). *National Systems of Innovation: Towards a Theory of Innovation and Interactive Learning*, London: Pinter Publishers.

Malta Ministry of Economic Services (1999). *Prosperity in Change: Challenges and Opportunities for Industry*, Malta: Ministry of Economic Services.

Marshall, D., Williams, G.B. and Collymore, C. (undated). 'A Study of Manufacturing Capabilities of Companies in the Eastern Caribbean', University of the West Indies, Barbados and University of Birmingham, UK, processed.

Matsis, S. (2001). 'Economic Growth and Development: Lessons from the Experience of Cyprus – A Small Island Economy', in Peretz, D., Faruqi, R. and Kissanga, E. (eds), *Small States in the Global Economy*, London: Commonwealth Secretariat, pp. 417–56.

Mauritius Employers Federation (2003). 'The Mauritian Textile and Clothing Industry', *EcoTrends*, July, No. 13. Cited as MEF (2003).

Metcalfe, S. (2003). 'Science, Technology and Innovation Policy', in G. Wignaraja (ed.), *Competitiveness Strategy in Developing Countries: A Manual for Policy Analysis*, London: Routledge.

Mytelka, L.K. (1999). *Competition, Innovation and Competitiveness in Developing Countries*, Paris: OECD.

McQueen, M., Philips, C., Hallam, D. and Swinbank, A. (1998). *ACP-EU Trade and Aid Co-operation*, Commonwealth, Economic Paper No 32, Commonwealth Secretariat: London.

OECD (1992). *Technology and the Economy: The Key Relationships*, Paris: OECD.

Porter, M.E. (1990). *The Competitive Advantage of Nations*, London: Macmillan Press.

Razzque, M.A. (2002). 'Small States in World Export Trade' in Commonwealth Secretariat, *Small States: Economic Review and Basic Statistics*, Vol. 7, Commonwealth Secretariat, London.

Radosevic, S. (1999). *International Technology Transfer and Catch-Up in Economic Development*, Cheltenham: Edward Elgar.

Streeten, P. (1993). 'The Special Problems of Small Countries', *World Development*, 21(2): 197–202.

Stiglitz, J.E. (2003). 'Globalisation, Technology and Asian Development', *Asian Development Review* 20(2): pp. 1–18.

Subramaniam, A. and Roy, D. (2001). 'Who Can Explain the Mauritian Miracle: Mead, Romer, Sachs or Rodrik?', *IMF Working Paper* No. 01/116.

Teal, F. (1999). 'Why Can Mauritius Export Manufactures and Ghana Not?', *World Economy* 22(7): 981–93.

Treebhoohun, N. (2001). 'The Mauritian Experience' in Peretz, D., Faruqi, R. and Kissanga, E. (eds), *Small States in the Global Economy*, London: Commonwealth Secretariat, pp. 457–79.

ul Haque, I. (1995a). 'Introduction' in ul Haque, I. (ed.), *Trade, Technology and International Competitiveness*, Washington DC: World Bank Economic Development Institute.

UNCTAD (various). *World Investment Report*, Geneva, UNCTAD

UNCTAD (2000). *Investment Policy Review: Mauritius*, Geneva, UNCTAD.

UNIDO (2002). *World Industrial Development Report 2002/2003: Competing Through Innovation*, Vienna: UNIDO.

UNDP (2003). *Human Development Report 2003*, New York: UNDP.

Wignaraja, G. (1997). 'Manufacturing Competitiveness With Special Reference to Small States' in Commonwealth Secretariat, *Small States: Economic Review and Basic Statistics*, Vol. 3, Commonwealth Secretariat, London.

Wignaraja, G. (1998). *Trade Liberalisation in Sri Lanka: Exports, Technology and Industrial Policy*, Basingstoke, UK: Macmillan Press.

Wignaraja, G. (2002). 'Firm Size, Technological Capabilities and Market-Oriented Policies in Mauritius', *Oxford Development Studies*, 30(1): 87–104.

Wignaraja, G. (2003a). 'Competitiveness Analysis and Strategy', in Wignaraja, G., *Competitiveness Strategy in Developing Countries*, London: Routledge.

Wignaraja, G. (2003b). 'Competitiveness, Productivity Management and Job Creation in African Enterprises: Evidence from Mauritius and Kenya', Management and Corporate Citizenship Working Paper No. 5, Job Creation and Enterprise Development Department, International Labour Office: Geneva.

Wignaraja, G. (forthcoming). 'Institutional Support and Policies for Technology Development in SMEs in Mauritius' in Oyenka, B. (ed.), *Innovation and the African Enterprise*, Cheltenham, UK: Edward Elgar.

Wignaraja, G. and Ikiara, G.K. (1999). 'Adjustment, Technology and Enterprise Dynamics in Kenya' in S. Lall (ed.), *The Technological Response to Import Liberalisation in Sub-Saharan Africa*, London: Macmillan Press and New York: St Martins Press.

Wignaraja, G. and O'Neil, S. (1999). *SME Exports and Public Policies in Mauritius*, Commonwealth Trade and Enterprise Paper No. 1, Commonwealth Secretariat: London.

Wignaraja, G. and Taylor, A. (2003). 'Benchmarking Competitiveness: A First Look at the MECI', in Wignaraja, G. *Competitiveness Strategy in Developing Countries*, London: Routledge.

Wint, A.G. (1996). 'Assessing the Export Competitiveness of Trinidad and Tobago: Lessons for Export Policy in Developing Countries', Kingston: University of the West Indies, mimeo.

Wint, A.G. (2003). *Competitiveness in Small Developing Economies: Insights from the Caribbean*, Kingston: University of West Indies Press.

Winters, L.A. and Martins, P.M.G. (2003). 'Beautiful But Costly: An Analysis of Operating Cost of Doing Business in Small Economies', London: Commonwealth Secretariat and Geneva: UNCTAD, mimeo.

Woldekidan, B. (1994). 'Export-led Growth in Mauritius', Indian Ocean Policy Paper 3, National Centre for Development Studies, Australian National University: Canberra.

World Bank (1994). *Mauritius: Technology Strategy for Competitiveness*, Report No. 12518-MAS, Washington DC: World Bank.

World Bank (1998). *Enhancing the Role of Government in the Pacific Island Economies*, East Asia and Pacific Region, Washington D.C: World Bank.

World Bank (2003). *World Development Indicators*, Washington D.C: World Bank.

Word Trade Organisation (1996), *Trade Policy Review: Mauritius 1995*, Geneva: World Trade Organisation.

Word Trade Organisation (1998). *Trade Policy Review: Trinidad and Tobago 1998*, Geneva: World Trade Organisation.

WEF (2003). *Global Competitiveness Report 2003*, New York: Oxford University Press for the World Economic Forum. *www.weforum.org*